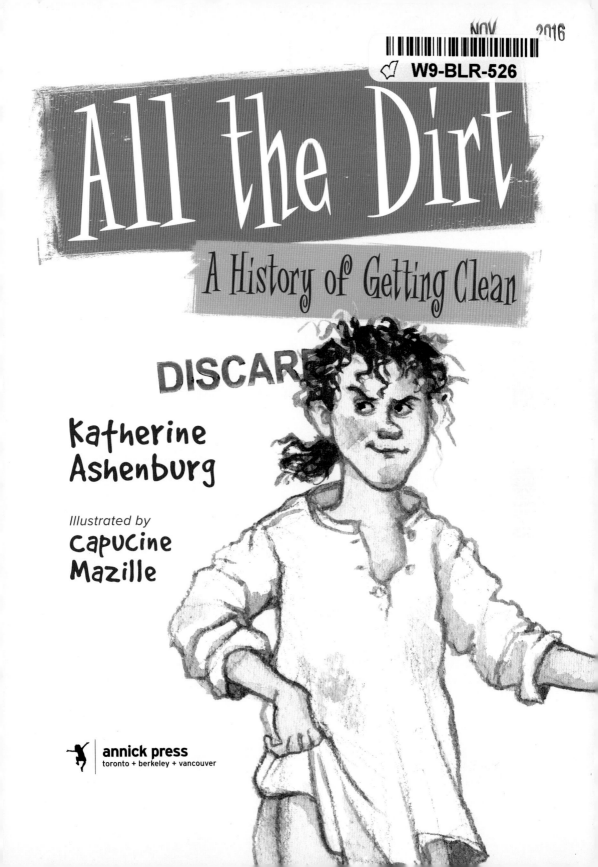

All the Dirt

A History of Getting Clean

Katherine Ashenburg

Illustrated by
Capucine Mazille

annick press
toronto + berkeley + vancouver

Cover art/design by Pixel Hive Studio
Edited by Barbara Pulling
Designed by Pixel Hive Studio

Annick Press Ltd.

We acknowledge the support of the Canada Council for the Arts, the Ontario Arts Council, and the participation of the Government of Canada/la participation du gouvernement du Canada for our publishing activities.

Cataloging in Publication

Ashenburg, Katherine, author

    All the dirt on getting clean / Katherine Ashenburg ; Capucine Mazille, illustrator.

Issued in print and electronic formats.

ISBN 978-1-55451-790-9 (bound).–ISBN 978-1-55451-789-3 (paperback).–
ISBN 978-1-55451-791-6 (epub).–ISBN 978-1-55451-792-3 (pdf)

    1. Hygiene–Juvenile literature. I. Mazille, Capucine, illustrator
II. Title.

RA780.A82 2016   j613'.4   C2016-900235-7
                                                C2016-900236-5

Published in the U.S.A. by Annick Press (U.S.) Ltd.
Distributed in Canada by University of Toronto Press.
Distributed in the U.S.A. by Publishers Group West.

Printed in China

Visit us at: www.annickpress.com

Also available in e-book format.
Please visit www.annickpress.com/ebooks.html
for more details. Or scan

Table of Contents

R0447280093

Introduction

Eight Myths About "clean"

Washing ourselves doesn't feed our hunger or quench our thirst or shelter us from the cold. So why do we do it? Kids might say, "Because our parents make us." Adults might say, "Because it makes a good impression" or "Because being clean is healthy." But throughout history, people around the world have washed themselves for all kinds of reasons, including to show respect to the gods, cure their ailments, and mark important changes in their lives.

At first glance, a country's bathrooms and bathhouses seem very ordinary. It's strange to think of them as windows into a people's values and dreams, but they are. People's attitudes toward dirt and cleanliness reveal a lot about the society they live in. And, since the earliest times, people had theories behind all the ways they washed themselves. Today, we know that a lot of those theories were wrong. But we still have many mistaken ideas—myths—about cleanliness. Here are some of the big ones.

MYTH #1
The definition of cleanliness is universal.

The funny thing about "clean"—and there are lots of funny things about it—is that most people believe they know what "clean" is and think that theirs is the only definition. Nothing could be further from the truth.

For an aristocratic seventeenth-century Frenchman, "clean" meant changing his linen shirt every day and dabbing his hands in water, but he never touched the rest of his body with water or soap. For a Roman woman in the first century, it meant two or more hours of splashing, soaking, and steaming her body in water of different temperatures, and raking off her sweat and oil with a metal scraper. She did this every day, with lots of other women around, and without using soap. In the southern African country of Zimbabwe, people don't feel clean until they coat their washed bodies with a mixture of oil and dirt. Along with your parents, the Frenchman, the Roman woman, and the Zimbabwean were each convinced that cleanliness was important and that their way was the royal road to a properly clean body.

MYTH #2
Cleanliness depends on modern technology.

It's true that plumbing and other engineering feats have made our modern Western standard of cleanliness possible, but what's much more important is whether people *want* to wash. The Roman bathhouses had clever heating and water-delivery systems that no one imitated for more than 13 centuries—because water was scary and washing wasn't a priority. Long before modern saunas, Aztecs and Navajos had figured out ways to enjoy steam baths.

MYTH #3
People were more or less filthy until around the start of the twentieth century.

Tell that to the ancient Egyptians, Aztecs, Chinese, and Greeks, who were pretty sensible about cleanliness, and to the Romans, who were extravagantly clean. Even medieval Europeans enjoyed a regular trip to the local steam bath. Especially in the West, there is no straight line of progress from "dirty" to "clean." It's all over the map.

MYTH #4
Doctors and scientists are the best sources of advice when it comes to cleanliness.

Not so—at different periods in history, some of the worst advice came from medical men and scientists. Even today, the experts don't always agree on how important it is to be sparklingly clean.

MYTH #5
Washing is something you do in private.

In the West, many of us do expect to be alone when we wash our naked bodies. But for the Romans, getting clean was a party! And it still can be for modern Indonesians, Turks, Finns, Hungarians, and other people around the world who wash in company.

MYTH #6
Getting yourself clean is a personal ritual with no connection to the larger world.

Cleanliness is closely connected to religion, culture, geography, and science, all around the world. It has been influenced by such things as the spread of Islam, the American Civil War, the Industrial Revolution, the worst plague ever, the abundance of hot springs in Japan, the discovery of the germ theory, the birth of advertising, the development of the American hotel, and much more. Exploring the history of cleanliness is kind of like seeing the history of the world through a soap bubble.

MYTH #7
Keeping your body clean is healthy.

Not so. Only one simple cleaning practice is important for your health. And you're going to have to read to the end of this book to find out what it is.

MYTH #8
Cleanliness is a nice, polite subject.

Wrong again. There's a lot that's gross about cleanliness. If you're squeamish, be forewarned—this book contains references to poop, bodily fluids, strong smells, and other shocking subjects. Have fun!

Chapter 1

Ancient Grime

3000 BCE TO 306 CE

Telemachus on Tour

PYLOS AND SPARTA, TWELFTH CENTURY BCE

Telemachus was miserable. His father, Odysseus, had left for the Trojan War when Telemachus was a baby. He'd been gone for 20 years, and no one knew where he was. Telemachus's house was filled with rude, violent men who wanted to marry his mother, Penelope. They ate his food, drank his wine, and sang their drunken songs all night. Telemachus hated these bullies, but he was young and awkward and didn't know how to get rid of them. The goddess Athena came to him in disguise and told him that his childhood was over; now he must be strong and go searching for his father. If he found that Odysseus was dead, Athena said, Telemachus must return home and kill his mother's suitors.

That was a scary task, but Athena filled the boy with confidence, and he sailed for Pylos, home of King Nestor. Nestor's mansion was everything Telemachus's disorderly house was not, and Nestor was the perfect host, ready with food, drink, a jug of water for hand-washing, and—above all—a bath. Important guests in ancient Greece were normally offered a bath when they arrived, as well as a servant to bathe them, but because his father was a famous king and warrior, Telemachus got extra-special treatment. The person who bathed him was none other than the king's youngest daughter, Polycaste, and she rubbed him with olive oil after the bath. Wearing a tunic that Polycaste had given him, Telemachus emerged from his bath as handsome as a young god. Everywhere he went, people noticed his resemblance to his father, but the boy also wanted to act like his father, resourceful and brave.

Next he traveled to Sparta, where King Menelaus and his queen, Helen, welcomed him. There, too, he was given a hot bath with all the trimmings, this time by servants. The courtesy and comfort of their palace and the respect they showed Telemachus left him with new poise. Now, in spite of the difficulties, he was determined to find his father and to rid his house of the bullies who wanted to marry his mother.

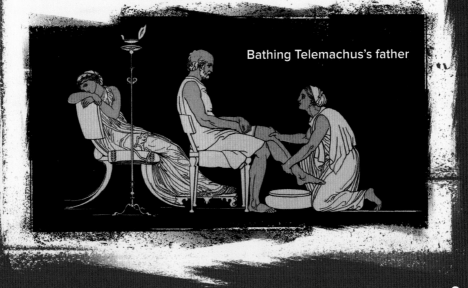

Bathing Telemachus's father

The Well-Washed Family

Telemachus and his parents, Odysseus and Penelope, are the main characters in Homer's great adventure story *The Odyssey*, which was written around 700 BCE. They are a very clean family, for reasons that would have been obvious to Greeks in Homer's lifetime. Greeks had to wash before praying and offering sacrifices to the gods, and in the story Penelope frequently begs the gods to return her husband and then her son. Greeks always bathed before setting out on a journey, and when they arrived at the house of strangers or friends, they would first be offered water to wash their hands, and then a bath. *The Odyssey* is a story full of arrivals and departures, as Telemachus searches for his father and Odysseus struggles to get home.

Homer loved describing the preparations for these baths—heating water in a copper container set on a tripod over a fire, and then pouring the hot water into a tub of brass or polished stone. His characters always look much, much better after a bath, sometimes even resembling gods—partly because *The Odyssey* is full of magic, but also because travelers on the hot, dusty roads of ancient Greece really did benefit from a good soak.

Washing, the Greek Way

By the fifth century BCE, if you were a boy or girl who lived in a comfortable house in Athens, with servants or slaves, you could clean yourself in various ways. Your house would probably have a washing room next to the kitchen. It would house a washstand that looked like a big birdbath, called a *labrum*. Using a jug or a basin, a servant would carry water from the tank that held

Taking the Plunge in Ancient India

In the Bronze Age, on the banks of the Indus River in what is now Pakistan and northwestern India, a peaceful and prosperous civilization grew up. Archaeologists call it the Indus Valley civilization. Cleanliness was important to the Indus Valley people, and most of their mud-brick houses had bathrooms and private wells. Wastewater from the bathrooms went into covered underground drains. Archaeologists can usually identify the bathroom in one of the surviving Indus Valley houses by the waste drains and the better-than-average quality of the brickwork.

In 1926, archaeologists excavating the Indus Valley city of Mohenjo-Daro discovered what may be the world's oldest public bath. Built around 3000 BCE, the pool measures 12 meters (39 feet) by 7 meters (23 feet), and is at its deepest at 2.4 meters (8 feet), about the size of a regular classroom. Many religions include washing and bathing in their ceremonies of purification and renewal, and scholars believe that this Great Bath, as it is called, was used for religious ceremonies.

the household's water or from the nearest well. He might fill the *labrum* with water, or just pour it over you. The washing room might also include a pottery hip bath—big enough for you to sit in, with legs straight out in front, but not to lie down in—which drained through a channel to the outside.

Keeping clean was harder for people without money or servants. Poor people might use the nearest well for a daily wash and make an occasional visit to the public bath. These baths were either free or had a very low admission price, so that everyone could afford to go.

Just What the Doctor Ordered

Doctors in ancient Greece didn't have much to offer in the way of medicine or safe surgery, so they often prescribed baths. Hippocrates, the great doctor from the fifth century BCE, was a champion of baths. He believed that a smart combination of cold and hot soaks could bring the body's humors, or liquids, into a healthy balance. Warm baths also helped the body by softening it, allowing it to absorb nourishment, and supposedly eased ailments from headaches to problems with peeing. Cold showers were prescribed for people with joint problems. Female ills were often treated with steam baths.

The Naked Place

Once a middle- or upper-class Greek boy became a teenager, he had another place where he could wash—the gymnasium. This was an important meeting place for Athenian boys and men, and its rooms bordered an outdoor exercise field, with a running track nearby. Greek males exercised in the nude—gymnasium means "the naked place"—first oiling their bodies and then covering them with a thin layer of dust or sand. After wrestling or running or playing ball games, they removed the oil and dust, now mixed with sweat, with a curved metal scraper called a strigil. You could scrape your chest, arms, and legs yourself, but you needed a friend or a servant to do your back. (The strigil had staying power: the Greeks used it for centuries, and the Romans took it up from them.) After a good  scraping, you got washed, either standing at a *labrum* or using a tub or shower. The shower was pretty low tech: the showerer stood under a hole in a wall, and a servant poured water through the hole.

Wimps versus Tough Guys

You probably don't think that bathing in warm water says much about you as a person. For the Greeks, it said a lot! They worried that washing with warm water would make men and boys weak and fussy. In his fifth-century BCE comedy *The Clouds*, the playwright Aristophanes makes fun of the tug-of-war in Athens between the tough guys who washed in cold water and those who liked pampering. One of his characters, Strepsiades, fondly remembers his grimy boyhood, a time when no one bothered him about washing or keeping tidy. Strepsiades admires men who never shave, get their hair cut, or wash at the baths, whom he compares to his son, who is "always at the baths, pouring my money down the plug-hole." A character called Fair Argument harks back to the good old days when boys sang rousing soldier songs and would have been embarrassed to cover their bodies in oil.

"Sit in my own dirty water? No thanks!"

Many people who shower think baths are gross because you're sitting in dirty water, and the ancient Egyptians agreed. They were a very clean people, especially the priests, who shaved their own bodies every day to prevent lice. Most middle- and upper-class Egyptians washed themselves several times a day—when they got up in the morning, and before and after the main meals—but they never sat in a tub. A slave would douse them with warm water from a basin or a jug in the bathroom, which had a drainage hole in the floor.

He complains about the current crop of boys, who shiver in the cold after their hot baths and waste their time gossiping.

Greece's two most important city-states, Athens and Sparta, could not have been more different. The Athenians admired athletes, but also thinkers and artists. Sparta had little time for anybody but soldiers and athletes.

The Spartans despised luxury and even normal comforts. Boys were taken from their parents at seven and toughened up in dormitories, walking without shoes and sleeping on scratchy reeds. They never got enough to eat, which meant they had to steal food—another part of their education. Spartan girls were trained in sports and military exercises, and were encouraged to mock boys who weren't good at those things. Does it sound likely that these kids would have taken hot baths? You're right. We know of no warm bathing—and not much bathing of any kind—in Sparta.

Pour in Wine, Then Add the Baby

Although the Spartans were not big on baths, they bathed their newborns in wine. Plutarch, a Greek historian, saw the practice as a test: a wine bath would throw sickly children into convulsions, he thought, but would harden and strengthen healthy children. Spartan mothers might also have had the idea that wine acted as an antiseptic, but no one today knows for sure. One thing is certain: the wine bath wasn't the newborn Spartan's only test. A committee came to inspect every baby, and if the infant looked weak, they would leave it to die on a hillside.

Three Bright Ideas

Roman families often visited the bathhouse together. If they were hungry after relaxing for a few hours in warm, hot, and then cold waters, people could go to the bathhouse hall, where various kinds of food were sold. Children might be given sips from their parents' honeyed wine as they downed mussels, boiled eggs with pine nut sauce, sausage, and a hot cheesecake called *libum*.

A day at the bathhouse was an excellent family outing, and several clever Roman inventions played a part in making it so much fun. Take, for example, the bathhouse's abundant water. In 312 BCE, the Roman leader Appius Claudius oversaw the building of the first Roman aqueduct, a stone channel that transported water from the Via Prenestina, a road in central Italy, 18 kilometers (11 miles) along the Appian Way to Rome. By 100 BCE, Rome had nine aqueducts that supplied almost a million cubic meters (35 million cubic feet) of water every day — that's 400 Olympic swimming pools! That provided each Roman with a daily allowance of 1,135 liters (300 gallons) — about three times the average used by a twenty-first-century North American!

Water was sent to the furnace by means of pumps and pipes, and then to the bath's various chambers. The water wasn't the only thing that was heated. The rooms of the baths were heated by a system called hypocaust, which means "a furnace that heats from below." The hypocaust heated a hollow space underneath the floors and behind the walls with hot air from the furnace. The floor could become very hot, so bathers protected their feet with wooden-soled sandals.

Early Roman baths had been made of squared stones. By the first century BCE, the invention of Roman concrete — a mixture of brick fragments and stones in a mortar of lime, sand, and volcanic dust — made vast, complicated buildings possible. The development of the concrete vaulted roof, in particular, helped create the huge spaces that made a visit to the imperial baths unforgettable.

Baths, Roman Style

The Greeks appreciated water, but the Romans adored it. For boys and men, a trip to a Roman bathhouse in the first century BCE would begin with the bather, naked and oiled, working up a light sweat in the exercise yard. Girls and women didn't use the exercise yard, but everyone bathed in waters in a series of different temperatures. First (after exercise for the males) came the tepidarium, a moderately warm room, where the bathers perspired and scraped off their oil, sweat, and dirt with a strigil. Pumice (light, porous rock) and fermented urine—lovely!—were two other cleansing aids. In the next chamber, the caldarium, the bather would plunge into a pool of hot water or sprinkle hot water on himself from a basin. Finally came the frigidarium, a room with a shockingly cold plunge pool. The plunge could be followed by another oiling, a massage, and a final scraping with the strigil.

This kind of neighborhood bath was comfortable, but the imperial baths—a gift from the emperor to the Roman people—were vast pleasure palaces. The first imperial bath, built by the emperor Agrippa in 25 BCE, was decorated with 300 statues and included an artificial lake. The Baths of Diocletian (built from 298–306 CE) had room for 3,000 bathers. In Rome, men, women, slaves, and children all used the baths. For the poor people who lived in the city's dark apartment blocks, the huge, light-filled imperial baths let them experience Rome at its most splendid. With its pools, exercise yards, gardens, libraries, meeting rooms, and snack bars, an imperial bath was a multipurpose place to hang out, do business, gamble, flirt, talk politics, eat, and drink. Oh yes, and bathe.

Earplugs, Please!

A bathhouse appealed to all the senses, from the smell of the oils to the feel of the water and the sight of the bathers, either naked or decked out in show-offy robes. But for the Roman writer Seneca, who lived over a bathhouse in the first century CE, it was all about the noise. He couldn't avoid the grunts of exercisers swinging their dumbbells, the obnoxious person who insisted on calling out the score of a game, the man who loved the sound of his own singing in the bath, the people who leaped into the pool with a huge, look-at-me splash, the cries of the sausage sellers and the pastry cooks. Two of the most gruesome sounds were connected to the depilator, a man who plucked the hair in people's underarms—another of the bathhouse services. The depilator advertised his work with a shrill cry, and the person being plucked added his or her own yell to the mix.

Everyone Out, Here Comes the Statue!

In the fifth century BCE, an upper-class man in China was expected to wash his hands five times a day, bathe every fifth day, and wash his hair every third day. (Men wore their hair long, so washing it was important.) In the second century BCE, Chinese emperors, like Roman emperors, enjoyed all kinds of fancy touches in their baths. The Chinese had one trick that would have surprised the Romans — to warm the water in a pool, they would heat a bronze statue red-hot and then throw it in!

On the Steamy Side

The Romans were not the only people in the ancient world to appreciate hot water and steam. At least as far back as 1000 BCE, the Japanese soaked in mineral-rich hot springs for their health. Volcanoes and mineral springs go together: with more than 100 volcanoes, Japan has 2,300 natural hot springs. The Japanese built simple outdoor baths at these springs, called *onsen*. When the first Buddhist monks came to Japan in 552 BCE, they quicly developed a belief that steam could cleanse the soul as well as the body. They began using *onsen* as part of their daily practice, hoping to wash away their sins and their attachment to the world.

On the other side of the world, Native Americans valued steam for the same reasons as the Japanese—to heal the body and revive the spirit. While the Romans were building their vast imperial baths, the Aztecs and the Mayans in Central America were constructing *temazcalli,* small round sweat lodges where steam was produced by heating bricks or stones. Small groups would enter the *temazcal,* enjoy the steam, and take a cold shower after leaving.

Farther north, Native American tribes such as the Navajos and Sioux built circular, temporary structures covered with animal skins. They produced steam either with hot rocks or by burning logs. These sweat lodges were believed to help people with

Bringing the sweat lodge willows

all kinds of physical problems, like broken bones and growths on the skin, as well as to aid in childbirth.

THE Story OF Soap
PART ONE

Archaeologists in Babylon, an ancient city in modern-day Iraq, found clay cylinders from about 2800 BCE that contain a soapy material. According to the writing on the cylinders, fat and ashes were boiled together to produce it. That sounds disgusting—and not at all clean—but that is how soap was made for most of human history. What actually got washed with this early soap is less clear, perhaps cloth or pots and pans. The Egyptians used animal fats, as well as milder vegetable oils, to make soap for washing their bodies.

Chapter 2

Saints, Steam, and Soap

307 TO 1550

Behind the Veil

CONSTANTINOPLE, 1500

Maryam and her mother were going to the neighborhood *hamam*, or bathhouse. Making her way carefully through the noisy, bustling market, Maryam's mother carried the henna she had mixed the night before— a vegetable dye she used to keep her hair red-brown—as well as drinks and fruit. Maryam carried their towels, combs, and clean clothes. It was one of the days set aside for women and girls to visit the *hamam*, as shown by a veil over the main door.

The *hamam* was filled with the cheerful sound of women and girls laughing and gossiping in the three main rooms. First came Maryam's favorite, the dimly lit *sicaklik*, or hot room. The walls were covered with tiles decorated in blue, green, and white geometric patterns, but the eye was drawn to the tiny, star-shaped openings in the dome.

Even though it was morning, it always seemed like a starlit evening in the *sicaklik*. Maryam loved poetry, and many famous poets had been inspired by this romantic space. She spotted her older cousin, Fatima, and once they were thoroughly hot, the two girls went on together to the *sogukluk*, the warm room. In this room, there was no pool. Instead, the *hamam* had attendants who washed the girls briskly with soap and water using a rough mitten.

Finally, the girls relaxed in the cool room, drinking tea and eating fruit and gooey, delicious pastries. In this room, the women visiting the *hamam* applied kohl to their eyes, dyed their hair and eyebrows with henna, and had their body hair removed with sharp-edged shells. Servants or attendants helped with the shells. The process made Maryam wince when she looked too closely.

Maryam's mother was busy with her henna, and her sister-in-law, Fatima's mother, was helping her. But she seemed oddly preoccupied.

"Why does my mother keep looking at that corner?" Maryam asked Fatima.

Fatima laughed. "Don't you know? She's looking at Layla."

Layla was an older teenager who lived nearby. Maryam watched her chatting with her friends while she practiced outlining her eyes with kohl.

"Your mother is thinking about Layla as a possible bride for your brother," Fatima added.

Maryam's eyes widened. She knew that one reason mothers came to the *hamam* was to consider which local girls might be suitable for their sons. Some mothers even made a point of talking closely with the older girls to see if any of them had bad breath. It hadn't occurred to her that Ahmet, her brother, was old enough to marry, or that her mother was on the lookout for the right bride. Now she looked at Layla with new eyes. Some of the older girls ignored Maryam and her friends, but Layla always greeted them warmly. "I hope Layla does marry Ahmet," Maryam whispered to her cousin. It was exciting to think that a girl she liked so much might soon be the newest member of their family.

The Baths Move East

The *hamam* where Maryam went with her mother may remind you in some ways of the smaller Roman neighborhood baths. The sporty part of the Roman bath—the exercise yard—had disappeared, and the rough mitten and soap had replaced the strigil, but there was a family resemblance between the *hamam* and its Roman ancestor.

But what happened to the Roman bath? The short answer is that the mighty Roman empire fell. In the fifth century CE, Germanic tribes plundered and raided Rome. In 476, the Roman emperor, Romulus Agustulus, was deposed by a Germanic chieftain called Odoacer. The Roman empire in the west was finished, although its eastern arm, the Byzantine empire, with its headquarters in Constantinople, continued for another thousand years.

The Romans called the Germanic tribes who invaded their empire barbarians because they weren't Romans: they didn't wear togas or speak Latin. The invaders didn't get the point of the Romans' beloved baths, either. Real men, in their view, did not hang out in steamy bathhouses; they took a quick dip in a stream, in late spring or summer, and marinated themselves in their own sweat for the rest of the year. Plus, they styled their hair with rancid butter, which, not surprisingly, smelled revolting to the Romans.

When the Goths, one of the Germanic tribes, disabled the Roman aqueducts in 537, that was the end of the imperial baths. Even if the aqueducts could have been repaired, Rome was too disorganized by then to manage the operations that supplied the imperial baths with water. That still left

more than 800 simple neighborhood baths in the capital, but within a few centuries, most of them also closed.

The baths lasted longer in the Byzantine empire, where the *hamam* was born. In the eastern provinces of Syria, Judaea, and Arabia, where Roman and Islamic traditions mingled, a hybrid developed. The bathers washed at basins rather than in pools, and the *hamam* centered on a large social hall. You can still wash at a *hamam* (also called a Turkish bath) in many parts of the world, and when you do, you're as close as you can come to taking a Roman bath.

Hands Off Our Cauldron

Buddhist monasteries and temples in Japan always had baths, for the use of the monks as well as the pilgrims and poor people who showed up at their door. The monks heated water for their baths in huge cauldrons, and these vessels were considered some of the monastery's treasures. When temples competed with each other, they sometimes took to stealing their rival's cauldrons!

In the eighth century, the Empress Koyo made a vow to bathe 1,000 beggars with her own hands. Having washed 999, she looked at the last beggar and saw that he had leprosy, which was considered very contagious at the time. The empress kept to her vow and bravely washed the man. Once she had finished, the leper revealed that he was the Buddha, the holy founder of Buddhism. The empress had passed his test.

Want to Be Holy? Stop Washing

In 380, Christianity, the new religion that began in the first century CE, was proclaimed the official religion of the Roman empire. If you were an early Christian, you could easily be confused about your body: Was it good or bad? Saints' bodies were considered so pure that parts of them worked miracles—their saliva, or a bit of bone housed in a special little shrine in a church could supposedly cure people. But if you weren't a saint, your body was likely to get you into trouble. Ignoring it as much as possible seemed like the way to go, which included not paying attention to how much you washed. Some very strict types, like St. Jerome, thought baths could make a girl conceited and take her attention away from God. He thought the well-behaved girl should spoil her looks by being messy and uncombed.

Things were particularly weird in the fourth and fifth centuries, when extreme dirtiness became a badge of holiness for Christians. If saintly people gave up good food, wine, and comfortable beds so that they could concentrate on God, then why not give up cleanliness, too? (Yes, odd as it seems when you don't feel like taking a shower, people at the time thought being clean was a pleasure—and a dangerous one at that.

Many early saints went out of their way to be filthy. St. Agnes was only 13 when she was either beheaded or stabbed to death in Rome for being a Christian—no one knows which for sure—but one of her claims to saintliness was that she had never washed any part of her body.

Godric, an English saint, walked from England to Jerusalem, a journey of more than 3,500 kilometers (2,175 miles), without once washing himself or changing his clothes. At home in the woods near Durham, he wore an itchy shirt made of hair. When the hair mixed with summertime sweat, it attracted lots of lice—which Godric welcomed, because, to serve God, he was trying to be as uncomfortable as possible.

THE Story OF Soap PART TWO

A thorough scrubbing with a rough goat-hair mitt and lots of soap was a standard part of the Turkish bath, or *hamam*. Soap makers in the Middle East had been experimenting with olive oil soaps at least since the seventh century, and one of their earliest successes came from Aleppo, Syria. Soap there was made from olive oil, lye, and oil from the laurel tree, which turned the cakes green. It's believed that the Crusaders brought Aleppo soap, or one of its close cousins, back to Europe in the eleventh century. Laurel trees were not available in Europe, but regions where olive oil was plentiful, such as Castile in Spain and Marseille in France, adapted the Aleppo formula and became known for their fine, hard soap. However, it was considered a luxury and taxed so heavily that most people couldn't afford it. Europeans still boiled animal fats and ashes together, which made a soap for washing clothes and floors, but it was too harsh for bodies. For washing themselves, they made do with plain water, to which they sometimes added herbs.

Many of these very dirty Christians were hermits, people who lived by themselves, far away from other people. One monk who was walking in the desert came upon a hermit in a cave. He reported later that he had "smelt the good odor of that brother from a mile away." The stinkier you were, the holier you were, so that was quite a compliment! St. Francis of Assisi was a big fan of dirt, and he is said to have appeared to monks after his death to congratulate them on their grubby cells. St. Etheldreda, a seventh-century Anglo-Saxon queen who founded a convent, dressed in woolen clothing all year round and washed in warm water only four times a year. Even then, she used only the dirty water left over from baths taken by her nuns.

Here Come the Spaniards: Where's the Incense?

The Aztec civilization in central Mexico was strikingly advanced. They grew their food in an intensive system called *chinampas*, or floating gardens; public service cleaners swept and watered the streets of their capital, Tenochtitlan, daily; and public toilets were built in every neighborhood. Montezuma, the Aztec king, washed twice a day, like most Aztecs, either in a lake, river, or *temazcal*, their sweat bath. Aztecs washed with the fruit of the soaptree and other lathering plants. They also used deodorants made from copal gum (sticky resin from the copal tree), balsam oil, and amber oil; breath fresheners made from chicle (the gum from the sapodilla tree); and teeth-cleaners, such as a mixture of honey and white ash.

Modern soap nuts used today

Into this clean land thundered the dirty, stinky Spaniards. In 1519, they invaded Tenochtitlan (now Mexico City). The washing habits of the Aztecs amazed them, as the Spaniards were among the most devoted anti-bathers of the time in Europe. Moors had occupied Spain from 711 to 1492, and the resentful Spaniards wanted to be as different from their conquerors as possible. Because the Moors, who were Muslims, liked cleanliness, the Spanish decided to be super-dirty. In self-defense, the Aztecs took to fumigating the Spaniards with incense as they approached. The Spaniards took it as a compliment, but the Aztecs did it to mask their smell.

A Steamy Homecoming

In 1095, Pope Urban II called for European Christians to invade the Holy Land (the area around Jerusalem associated with the life of Jesus) and seize control of it from the Muslims. The Crusaders, as they were called, weren't successful. But they returned home from the Arab world with cool things that were new to Europe, including sugar, apricots, dates, chess, and carpets. They discovered something else they thought was really fun—the Turkish bath—and introduced that to Europeans, too.

The first medieval bathhouses combined a steam bath and, usually in a separate room, round wooden tubs that could seat six. Kids and adults went to the baths together every week or two. First they'd enjoy the steam, then the whole family would soak in one of the wooden tubs. Because sitting in hot water reminded people of cooking, in England they called the baths "the stews." If your town had a natural hot spring, as at Baden in Switzerland, a large outdoor bath that held dozens of people could be built over the spring.

The baths were hugely popular. They also encouraged naughty behavior, like drunkenness and fighting, which was part of their appeal. Whether or not you bathed naked depended on where you lived. Germany and Switzerland, where the baths were especially beloved, were okay with nakedness. Italy and the southern countries were not, so people from there were shocked when they visited north of the Alps.

An Italian doctor who lived in Germany scolded his neighbors for allowing families, from the littlest kids to the parents, to walk naked and near-naked through town on their way to the baths. An Italian traveler who went to the big outdoor bath at Baden was startled to see that windows had been cut into the partitions that separated the boys and men from the girls and women, so they could visit with each other. Horrors!

Pass the Arsewisp, Please

Even if your town had bathhouses, a steam and a tub soak every few weeks, without soap, was not going to keep you sweet-smelling for long. St. Thomas Aquinas thought that burning incense in church was a good idea, because it covered up the churchgoers' stink.

The part of the body people washed most often was their hands, and that made sense, as food was often eaten without a fork. There were no toothbrushes, so people in Wales rubbed their teeth with green hazel twigs and woolen cloths. That might not sound very effective, but it made people smell better than they did in Spain, where they brushed their teeth with pee!

Speaking of pee, there were urinals at St. Paul's, a boys' school in London that opened in 1509. But only urinals. When it came to pooping, the boys were told to go down to the nearby River Thames and use the river or the shore. When they needed to wipe themselves, they grabbed a handful of straw or hay, which they called an "arsewisp."

The Black Death

The Black Death, an outbreak of bubonic plague that killed between 30 and 60 percent of Europeans, was named for the dark, pus-filled lumps that appeared in the armpits, neck, and groin of its victims. For centuries, it was believed that rats carried the plague from Asia to Europe, and the fleas that lived on the rats transported it to humans. Now some scientists believe that the disease was airborne and passed from human to human.

Beginning in 1347, the Black Death invaded Italy, Spain, France, England, Germany, Austria, and Hungary.

Houses OF Perfumed Water

By the eleventh century, China had commercial bathhouses, which were called perfumed-water establishments. If you saw a water pot or kettle hanging outside a building, you knew you had arrived at a bathhouse. When the great Italian traveler Marco Polo reached the city of Hangzhou late in the thirteenth century, he found a city of 3,000 baths built on hot springs. The Chinese, he reported, went to the baths several times a month.

At the baths, you could pay a back-scrubber to give you a massage. A poem from the eleventh century goes like this:

A word for the masseur:
You have been working hard all day,
elbows in action.
Take it easy on me!
A scholar in retirement isn't dirty.

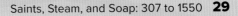

"Cleanliness Is Half the Faith"

Unlike Europeans in the early Middle Ages, the people of India were encouraged to be clean. India's two main religions, Hinduism and Islam, stressed the importance of cleanliness and insisted that people wash, for example, before entering a temple (Hinduism) or praying (Islam). Muhammad, the founder of Islam, said, "Cleanliness is half the faith." Plus, washing yourself in cool water was a relief in India's extreme heat, so Indians tried to bathe at least once a day and sometimes more often. Medieval paintings and statues from Karnataka, a state in southwestern India, show scenes of everyday cleanliness, including a man being helped to wash his long hair, a woman having an oil bath and shampoo, and women enjoying a large bathing pool.

There were so many deaths from the Black Death that the bodies were buried each morning in mass graves without coffins, covered only by a layer of earth. Next morning, hundreds more corpses were buried, followed by a fresh layer of dirt. The awful sight reminded one observer in Florence of a favorite dish—the alternating layers of bodies and earth, he wrote, were "just as one makes lasagne with layers of pasta and cheese."

With 25 million deaths in 1347–48, people were terrified. King Philippe VI of France consulted the medical experts at the University of Paris. Saturn, Jupiter, and Mars had collided, the doctors reported to the king, causing toxic vapors and making the air poisonous to breathe. Who was most vulnerable, according to the doctors? People who were fat, emotional, drank too much alcohol or . . . took hot baths! They said that once the plague entered the body through pores

Stepping toward Clean

Conserving water during the dry season was a problem in the northern Indian states of Rajasthan and Gujarat. People solved the problem with a unique structure called the stepwell. The well could be as deep as 30 meters (100 feet) and included pools for rainwater, fancy staircases, statues, arches, columns, and other decorations. People used the stone stepwells, some of which were 13 stories high and had 3,500 steps, for bathing, drinking water, and gathering together. It's thought that 3,000 of them were built, and hundreds still exist.

that had been opened by hot water, the person was doomed. The doctors were wrong, but that was the best medical opinion of the day.

In Europe, the plague was the beginning of the end for bathhouses. Whenever the disease returned, as it did at various times over the next four centuries, the cry went out: "Bathhouses and bathing, I beg you to shun them or you will die." Most baths closed their doors permanently, and people developed a morbid fear of water.

Chapter 3

It's a Foul, Foul World

1550 TO 1715

Drama at the Palace

MARLY, FRANCE, AUGUST 1705

Dearest Marie-Thérèse,

Parting from you was difficult—and we did have a lovely visit, didn't we?—but the journey here was atrocious! The way was hot and dusty, and so much dirt entered my open carriage it surprised me that any was left on the road. I arrived at the palace covered in dust and sweat. To make matters worse, I was late, and you know how His Majesty hates it when someone is tardy for dinner.

I went to my rooms in a panic, and Toinette, my maid, rushed to change my underwear and my dress. That made me presentable below the neck, but my face! Honestly, it looked as if I were wearing a gray mask. And there are no clean clothes with which to cover a dirty face.

Toinette just stared at me in dismay: we didn't know what to do.

And then I made a decision. There was no way around it. I would have to wash my face.

Toinette was startled, but she did as I asked and ran to fetch a saucer of water. Then, very carefully, she dipped a handkerchief in the water and blotted my face. I must admit, it made all the difference. I looked quite normal, and made it to dinner at the very last minute.

What an adventure! But please, no more of these dramas. It cannot be good for the heart to race like that.

With every good wish and thanks again for a delightful time in Paris,

Elisabeth Charlotte,
Princess Palatine

The Dirt Behind the Drama

You probably wash your face every day, if not more often. It wouldn't occur to you to mention such a boring event on Snapchat or Twitter, or to think of it as an adventure. But at the start of the eighteenth century in France, washing your face was a very big deal. (Note that the princess didn't wash her dirty body at all, just jumped into clean clothes. More on that later.)

Outsmarting THE Devil
[OR HOTTER THAN HELL]

Finnish children were often told a folktale about a farmer who adored the sauna. His reputation for loving heat reached Hell, and the Devil made a trip to Earth to tempt him. "Let me take you to a place where it is so hot," he said, "that you'll be begging me to stop it." Nothing could have pleased the farmer more, so the two went off to Hell. The Devil ordered more wood and coal for his huge fire, and soon Hell was ablaze. The extraordinary heat made volcanoes erupt on Earth, and polar ice caps melted. But the farmer loved it and kept thanking the Devil for his generosity. The Devil got more and more frustrated and angry: no matter what he did, he couldn't make it too hot for this dumb farmer. Finally, he yelled, "Out with you! I never want to see you here again." The farmer went back to Earth, sorry to miss the wonderful heat, but happy that he was not going to be damned to Hell.

The fact that people like the Princess Palatine hardly ever washed didn't mean they didn't care how they looked. Quite the opposite: at the French court, people worked hard to look as stylish and elegant as possible. But underneath their rich velvets and silks, their lace collars and glittering jewelry, were bodies that stayed unwashed from one year to the next. Hands were cleansed with water (no soap); the mouth might be rinsed quickly; and the face wiped with a dry cloth. That was usually it. Kids and grown-ups, from the richest to the poorest, teemed with lice, nits, and fleas. These critters were so common that no one was embarrassed about them.

Doctors of the time still believed blocking your pores with dirt was the best way to seal yourself off from infection. Even when the plague wasn't threatening, doctors saw baths as dangerous: they filled the head with vapors and loosened nerves and ligaments. The moral? Sensible people stayed away from water.

Please Get off My Shoulder Blades

Travel, they say, broadens the mind. When Europeans traveled outside the continent, they found it could also affect your body. Leonhard Rauwulf, a German doctor who visited Tripoli, Libya, in the 1570s, went to a public bathhouse. After sweating in a steam bath, he had a grueling massage that ended with Rauwulf lying on his stomach while the masseur stood on his shoulder blades. Next, an attendant applied a scary mixture of arsenic, quicklime (a corrosive chemical), and water to remove some of Rauwulf's body hair. Finally, using a rough cloth made of rope fibers, the attendant washed Rauwulf all over with soap made from olive oil. For the Muslims of Tripoli, this was a normal bathhouse visit. For the German doctor, it was a shocking, once-in-a-lifetime experience.

Don't Try This at Home Alone

Recommending that sick people do something considered dangerous for healthy people may sound silly, but European doctors believed a carefully supervised bath was sometimes a sick person's last chance. A bath was still considered a high-risk business, not something to try unless you had a doctor in charge.

On a spring day in 1610, King Henri IV of France sent a messenger to the Paris house of the Duc de Sully, France's superintendent of finances, asking that Sully report to the palace. To the messenger's shock, Sully was taking a bath when he arrived. Sully prepared at once to obey the king, but his servants begged him not to risk his health by going outside. Even the messenger was against it, assuring Sully that if the king "had known that you were in such a situation, he would have come here himself."

The messenger went back to the palace to explain the problem. The king took it as seriously as everyone else and consulted the royal doctor, who said that Sully would be in delicate health for several days to come.

Inueni vnam preciosam margaritam quam inti mo corde collegi :~

The king commanded Sully not to leave his house. He sent word that he would visit Sully at home the next day, and that he expected to find him in his nightshirt, leggings, slippers, and nightcap, "so that you come to no harm as a result of your recent bath." Normally, His Majesty didn't travel to his ministers' houses, much less order them to receive him in their nightclothes, but a bath was no normal event.

Hardworking Linen

In 1576, an Italian musician named Hieronymus Cardanus complained that the men and women around him "swarmed with fleas and lice, that some stank at the armpits, others had stinking feet, and the majority were foul of breath." That pretty much summed it up for the sixteenth century. But the seventeenth century raised the bar: it was awesomely dirty, maybe the dirtiest century of all in Europe.

Taking Cleanliness Seriously

Visitors to Japan, from the Chinese in the third century to the Europeans in the sixteenth century, frequently commented on how important cleanliness was to the Japanese. Even their language shows how seriously they took it: *fuketsu* means not only unclean but hideous; *kirei*, or clean, is a synonym for pretty; *kitani* is the word for dirty, but also for mean and nasty.

While doctors in the West were still advising people to avoid water for the sake of their health, Japanese doctors were investigating which minerals in their hot springs might help specific health problems. Samurai warriors favored mineral springs that were rich in gypsum to heal their wounds. In 1709, Goto Konzan, a doctor from Edo (now Tokyo), began the first medical study of hot baths.

When the French king Louis XIV woke up in his palace, a servant sprinkled a little rubbing alcohol on the king's hands. The king rinsed his mouth and wiped his face, and that was the end of his washing. You might guess from this that Louis spent most of the day sitting on his throne. Not at all: he was an athletic type who fenced, danced, and did military exercises so furiously that he would return to his bedroom in a sweat. But he still didn't wash; it was by putting on fresh clothes, and especially a white linen shirt, that Louis XIV became "clean." He was considered especially well groomed because he changed his shirt three times a day.

For the seventeenth century, clean linen was not a substitute for washing the body with water—it was better than that, safer and based on "science." People believed that white linen attracted and absorbed sweat. When they saw a grimy ring on the inside of their collar and cuffs, they thought the linen had removed all their dirt and made them clean.

The hardworking linen was fashioned into a long shirt, in the case of a boy or man, and more like a slip or chemise for a girl or woman. Linen became the clearest signal you could send that you were clean, and so more and more of it started to show. The sleeves of men's jackets were slashed so that the linen shirt poked through, and jackets were cut deliberately short to let the shirt balloon out at the bottom. The necks of women's dresses were scooped lower, so that the ruffles of their chemise showed, and the long sleeves of the chemise stretched beyond the dress sleeves as well.

Kings, Queens, and Peasants

Historians have discovered a lot more about kings, queens, and nobles from the past than about poor people. Most people couldn't write or read, so they didn't keep journals or write letters that were passed down through time. Almost no one thought poor people were important, so few outsiders were interested in writing about

THE Poor Man's Pharmacy

When travelers to Finland saw naked men in an extremely hot hut lashing themselves with branches, they found it very weird. For the Finns, it made perfect sense. Their beloved sauna bath involved heating a small building with a wooden fire to a temperature between 80 and 110 degrees Celsius (176 to 230 degrees Fahrenheit). They struck themselves with branches to increase their sweat, and when they couldn't bear the heat, they ran out into the snow or doused themselves with water. And then they returned to the hut for another round of heat, then cold.

Finns used the sauna for cleanliness, for companionship, and for health. The smoke lined its walls with a bacteria-resistant soot, and the Finns said the sauna was "the poor man's pharmacy." Because it was the cleanest place they had, Finnish babies were regularly born there and dead people were washed and laid out in the sauna.

them or their habits. Nobles and rich people, on the other hand, could usually read and write; plus, they had power, so other people recorded more about their lives. It's a safe bet, however, that the poor people in a society were never any cleaner than the rich. What makes this time in Western history unusual is that, since the fanciest doctors thought dirt protected you from disease, kings and queens were as dirty as the poorest peasant.

A Little More Sweat in the Wedding Cake, Please

Washing out the old and washing in the new is a natural way to mark an important life change. People all over the world, from ancient Greece to modern Africa, take a special bath around important occasions—a wedding, for example, or a birth or death. The place where Russians took this ceremonial bath was the *banya*, a sweat bath very similar to the Finns' sauna. The pre-wedding bath in the *banya* had a twist all its own. First, milk was poured over the bride's sweaty body, which was then coated with flour. After the resulting mess was scraped off, it was added to the wedding breads and cake! Go figure. That wasn't the only use for the bridal sweat: it was also mixed with vodka, wine, and grains and poured over the *banya*'s hot rocks.

Dirty Days

In Europe in the eighteenth century, baths continued to be pretty unusual events. People lived closely with each other's dirt and excrement. In Italy, people peed and pooped without embarrassment on staircases and landings and in courtyards. Shortly before King Louis XIV of France died in 1715, a new rule ordered that feces left in the hallways of the Palace of Versailles be removed once a week. (This was not dog poop, but human droppings.) Ordinary people emptied their chamber pots into the street, so passersby commonly dodged offerings from the windows above.

THE Patriotic Chemise

Princess Isabella, the daughter of King Philip II of Spain, became a national heroine when she vowed in 1601 not to change her chemise until the Siege of Ostend was over. Three years, three months, and thirteen days later, Spain took the city of Ostend from the Netherlands, and Isabella could change her underwear. Her originally white chemise had turned tawny colored by then.

Chapter 4

Some Like It Cold

1715 TO 1800

How to Bring Up an English Boy ... Brrrr

LONDON, FEBRUARY 1720

"Tom! Where have you gone?"

Tom was hiding in the attic. It was strictly off limits for him, but Mary, the family's maid, was busy in the kitchen, and Tom hoped his parents would not think of the attic.

"Tom, Dr. Locke is calling!"

It was one of his parents' favorite jokes, and a really bad one. Dr. Locke wasn't calling, but John Locke, who was a doctor and someone his father thought was very wise, had written a book about bringing up a boy. One of Dr. Locke's ideas was that boys should have their legs and feet immersed every day in colder and colder and colder water, to toughen them up. In winter, the barrel of water that Tom's mother left in the yard every night sometimes had a skin of ice on top, and Tom had to shatter it with his bare feet before he plunged in up to his knees.

"Tom! Mary has moved the barrel into the kitchen. Come straight downstairs."

Another of Dr. Locke's bright ideas was to dress boys in very thin shoes so that, in London's rainy climate, the shoes would leak and let in more cold water. Tom had spent many miserable days that winter in soggy shoes, feeling sure that he would never be warm again. Why didn't his sister, Cecily, have to undergo this daily misery? He heard his mother sighing with irritation as she trudged up the stairs to the attic. He flattened himself behind the door, but he knew it was no good. His mother would find him in an instant, and then the cold-water torture would begin.

More Than a Pinch of Salt

The book that made Tom's life miserable was called *Some Thoughts Concerning Education*, written in 1693. Dr. Locke wasn't interested in cleanliness; he believed that icy-cold water would harden boys and strengthen them.

Before people in England could begin to wash again, they had to overcome their fear of water, which had gone on for 400 years. Doctors like Locke had been gradually persuading people that you could immerse yourself in water and not come down with a serious disease. From plain water, doctors moved on to recommend sea bathing, in salt water. That, too, was weird advice in the early eighteenth century. Europeans waded and swam in rivers and lakes, but the ocean terrified them—it was huge, unpredictable, and the home, they thought, of horrible monsters.

In 1750, Dr. Richard Russell published a bestselling book that promised seawater was a miracle cure for glandular problems. Russell built a grand house overlooking the English Channel in Brighton. His patients had to bathe in the freezing cold sea at 5 a.m.; then they might be massaged with seaweed and showered with hot seawater. Sometimes the cure seemed worse than the disease. For patients who had trouble pooping, Russell prescribed drinking a pint of the salty water, which he said would produce "three or four sharp stools"!

The Race Is to the Coldest

The History of Cold Bathing (1701) claimed that cold water could cure just about any disease, and even turn losers into winners. One of its authors, Edward Baynard, noted something you might want to try: after two boys ran a race, if the loser was dipped in cold water and the boys ran the race again, the loser always won.

How to Bring Up a French Boy ... Brrrr

Across the English Channel, the French were also overcoming their resistance to water. Their guiding light was a writer named Jean-Jacques Rousseau, who believed that cleanliness was an essential part of the purity and naturalness he experienced in the countryside. (People who knew real farm life better than Rousseau agreed country people were "natural"— but also dirty and stinky.) In 1762, Rousseau published *Emile*, another book about the best way to bring up a boy. "Wash your children often," he wrote. "Their dirty ways show the need of this." Like Locke, Rousseau believed in bathing boys in icy-cold water, in winter and summer, but he also believed in cleanliness. If your parents tried to bring you up according to Rousseau's ideas—and many parents did—there was one piece of good news: you would never have to see a doctor. Rousseau thought that hygiene, or cleanliness, was "the only useful part of medicine."

How to Bring Up a Girl ...
Cleaner than Clean

When Emile, the main character in Rousseau's book, grows up, he chooses a partner, a girl named Sophy. To say that cleanliness is a big part of Sophy's personality is an understatement. In fact, Sophy's cleanliness is an obsession. She dislikes cooking, because "things are never clean enough for her," and gardening, because the manure heap used for fertilizer smells bad. Keeping her body, clothing, and room absolutely clean takes half of Sophy's time and, as Rousseau wrote, she thought "less of how to do a thing than of how to do it without getting dirty."

You might find that extreme. But Rousseau didn't think Sophy's cleanliness was exaggerated. He praised Sophy for not wearing perfume and said her husband would never find anything sweeter than her breath. Sophy, for him, was like nature itself—or at least like the sweet-smelling, impossibly perfect natural world imagined by Rousseau.

THE Nasty Secrets OF Perfume

French people who could afford it used perfume to mask their bad smells or those of their neighbors. Perfumes in the seventeenth and eighteenth centuries were based on animal secretions. Civet came from the anal glands of a wild, catlike mammal. (Eww.) Ambergris came from the intestines of a sperm whale. Musk was a secretion taken from the abdomen of a male musk deer. After the French Revolution, perfumes became lighter and were based on flowers.

Down with Dirt

For most of the seventeenth and eighteenth centuries, natural was the last thing the lords and ladies at the French court wanted to be. They covered their hair with wigs that were sometimes a foot high and hid their skin under oils, rouge, and powder. They wore unwashable brocades (rich silks with raised patterns), velvets, and satins that had permanent sweat stains under the arms.

In 1775, Queen Marie Antoinette sat for her portrait. In it, her powdered hair is built up to a dizzying height and threaded with pearls, ribbons, diamonds, and feathers; her hips are padded so that they stand out about a foot on either side of her waist. Eight years later, the queen sat for another portrait. If you'd only known her from the first picture, you wouldn't have recognized her. In the second portrait, her loose hair is only lightly powdered, and she wears a plain white cotton dress and a casual straw hat.

What happened? Times were changing across the continent, and clean and natural were now more fashionable than fancy and artificial. Following Rousseau's ideas about the simple life, Marie Antoinette had a little farm built for herself, complete with a herd of Swiss cows. The outfit she wears in the second portrait was perfect for her toy farm.

Tastes changed even more after the French Revolution, a 10-year struggle that included the execution of Marie Antoinette and her husband, Louis XVI, and led France toward democracy. Wigs, powdered hair, and heavy makeup reminded people of the hated royalty they had overthrown. Clean hair, shining faces, and washable cotton clothes looked modern, and much more attractive.

Rule, Britannia

Most of the champions of the cold bath were English. The English took the lead in other things, too, with a few brave people installing running water in their houses and indoor toilets instead of outhouses. A toilet was known in France as the "*lieu à l'anglaise*," or "the English place." The owner of an inn in Nimes, France, installed one to please her English customers, but not everyone got its point. A disgusted English visitor wrote that the French didn't use the seat but "left their offerings on the floor."

As the English got more keen on cleanliness and privacy, they often felt superior when they traveled abroad. An English traveler named Arthur Young went to the opera in Venice in 1789 and reported a shocking sight. A well-dressed man, Young wrote, had stepped into the small space between the orchestra and the audience, under the noses of some ladies, and then peed right onto the floor. Young added that he was the only one in the theater who seemed surprised: "It is, however, a beastly trick," he concluded.

And yet, lots of educated, prosperous Britons were not impressed with the new fashion for cleanliness. James Boswell, a writer from the Scottish upper class, almost never washed, and his stinkiness was famous. The Duke of Norfolk's servants bathed the duke only when he was too drunk to notice. When he was sober, he never washed more than his hands and face. When the ladies departed from the dining room, which was the tradition in smart English houses, the gentlemen could open a door in the sideboard, or a sliding panel in the wall, take out a chamber pot, and relieve themselves without interrupting the conversation.

Murder in the Bath

Jean-Paul Marat, a fiery leader of the French Revolution, spent a lot of time in his boot-shaped bath, where medicinal herbs helped to soothe his skin disease. He was working there on July 13, 1793, when a young woman named Charlotte Corday, who supported the royalist cause, stabbed him to death with a kitchen knife. She was beheaded by the guillotine four days later. If you visit the Musée Grévin (wax museum) in Paris, you can see the fatal knife and the copper-lined tub where Marat died.

Don't Make Me Look!

As people washed themselves more often, those who could afford a servant began to use portable bathtubs. These tubs were made of tin or copper, and in France, they were shaped like a boot. A servant would lug the tub into the bedroom, place it in front of the fire, and then fill it with water.

East Meets West

The women's *hamam* in Sofia, Bulgaria, was a lively, cozy place, furnished with cushions, carpets, and marble benches. It was filled with naked women chatting, drinking coffee, or eating sorbet, being washed and shampooed, and having their hair braided. One day in the mid-eighteenth century, the *hamam* had an unusual visitor—a young Englishwoman who was covered from neck to toe in formal riding clothes. It was Lady Mary Wortley Montagu, the wife of the English ambassador to Constantinople. The hospitable ladies of Sofia insisted that she must take off her clothes and enjoy the steam. While Lady Mary hesitated, one woman unbuttoned the visitor's top and exposed her complicated corset, an undergarment whose long strips of whalebone gave a strict shape to Lady Mary's body. Shocked, the Bulgarian woman ran to the other women and exclaimed that husbands in England tied up their wives in little boxes. The poor English ladies!

Many girls and women, especially, felt shy about having their nakedness exposed while washing. One solution was to cloud the bath water with bran or flour dissolved in alcohol. (That sounds messy!) More often, women and girls wore a special bathing dress. Marie Antoinette had breakfast every morning in her bath, wearing a long-sleeved flannel gown. When Elizabeth Montagu was staying at the Duke of Portland's grand house, she searched high and low for a bathtub. When she finally found one, she wrote to her mother, "Pray, look for my bathing dress, till then I must go in in *chemise* and *jupon!*"—in other words, her underwear.

Report from a Mikveh

Like Islam and Hinduism, Judaism saw cleanliness as a duty. One of the first things Jews built when they moved to a town was a special bath called a mikveh. Rabbis and religious men bathed there on the eve of the Sabbath and other holidays, and women bathed after menstruation and childbirth. Even dishes and pots and pans that had been made by non-Jews had to be purified in the mikveh before they touched food.

The mikveh was more about religious purity than physical cleanliness, but you had to be perfectly clean before you got into the mikveh. Some mikvehs, especially the pre-mikveh bath, became so pleasurable that rabbis reminded women they weren't supposed to be fun; they were an obligation. Not all mikvehs were such a treat, however. When a French traveler visited a mikveh in Frankfurt, Germany, in 1705, he was shocked to learn that women had to completely submerge themselves in the freezing cold water, so that every single hair was purified. The Frenchman wrote, "I am sure one can't stay long in this Bath without perishing."

Chapter 5

Baths and How to Take Them

EUROPE, 1800 TO 1900

A Maid's Afternoon on the Ringstrasse

COLOGNE, GERMANY, 1890

Today I accompanied Frau Mesmer and little Marta to the bathhouse. On our way there, we walked along the Ringstrasse, admiring the grand mansions and the Opera House, which looks magnificent from the outside. I have never seen the inside. I'm sure few maids have. The bathhouse is very close to the Opera House, and Frau Mesmer says that's because bathing is as important as great music.

Stuttgart's bathhouse has a bath for dogs as well as for people. Some people here in Cologne think that is silly, while others think we should have the same feature. Frau Mesmer says Cologne's bathhouse is so splendid that she should be able to bring Mitzi, her little dog, to enjoy it, too.

Marta's description of the inside of the main bathhouse makes me long to see its murals, its decorative glass, and the poetry painted on the walls. But I can only go to the People's Swimming Bath, which is very plain. Frau Mesmer tells me swimming in cool water is the best way for the poorer classes to get clean, and it costs less than the least expensive kind of bath in the main bathhouse. We must enter the People's Swimming Bath through a separate entrance at the back of the building.

Marta is only nine, but she is a sensitive girl. Once we are in sight of the bathhouse, she pulls her mother's arm to bring her down to her level and whispers in her ear. Frau Mesmer is not so sensitive, and she answers loudly, as she does each time Marta makes this request.

"Marta, that is completely impossible. It's forbidden, and besides, Else would not want to join us. She would feel very awkward in our bath."

At the carved front doors that flank the main entrance, I hand Frau Mesmer the basket with the special creams and soaps she and Marta use. As I turn the corner of the building and head toward the forbidding-looking door to the People's Swimming Bath, Marta gives me a sad little wave.

The Return of Water...
Gradually

Bathing was such a lost art in the nineteenth century that a doctor, Harriet Newell Austin, actually wrote an article called "Baths and How to Take Them." People were looking for guidance. After more than 400 years of advising that water was dangerous, scientists had now decided that clean skin was good, because it allowed carbon dioxide to leave the body through open pores. They were wrong about that, since carbon dioxide exits when we breathe out, but they did experiments on animals that convinced them that blocked pores could be deadly. Horses whose hides were shaved and then tarred died slowly. If they added glue to the tar, death came more quickly. Other poor animals were coated with varnish, and also died. We now know that these deaths were caused more by loss of thermal control than respiratory problems, but the scientists who did the experiments managed to convince people that regular washing with water was healthy.

This was a revolutionary idea, and people took their time accepting it. Take, for example, the master of a college at Cambridge University. When someone suggested that baths be provided for the students, he said no. There was no need, he explained, since "these young men are with us only for eight weeks at a time."

Sidewalk Showers

Until the 1840s, boys and men in France and other European countries peed on sidewalks, roads, and buildings. Then the Parisians introduced public urinals called pissoirs, small buildings on the street where you could pee in privacy and the urine would go into the sewers. This bright idea inspired a German doctor: Why not provide showers on the street too? In 1883, Dr. Oscar Lassar designed a corrugated iron "People's Bath" meant for the sidewalk, which held five shower stalls for men and five for women. A nozzle mounted high on the wall in each stall sprayed warm water.

Fans of the "rain bath," as the shower was called, crowed that it was the cheapest, simplest, and quickest way to clean yourself. But the iron shower houses never caught on. People at the time found it weird enough just to stand naked under water, let alone doing it in a public stall.

Baths To Go

In 1819, Parisians got a new way to bathe. A service called a *bain à domicile*, or "bath at home," delivered everything you needed—a tub, a robe, a sheet for drying, and hot, cold, or tepid water as ordered. Imagine the work of carrying all that equipment up several flights of stairs and then, when the bath was over, whisking it all away. The water usually disappeared through a hose that ran from the tub to the gutter on the street. A favorite practical joke involved ordering several baths to be delivered in the middle of a friend's dinner party. But however much people enjoyed talking about the *bains à domiciles*, only 1,000 were ordered in 1838, when more than a million people lived in Paris.

Close Encounters of an Unhealthy Kind

While the middle and upper classes were starting to clean themselves up, poor people were becoming even dirtier. In Britain, hundreds of thousands of people left the countryside to work in the new manufacturing cities. After a long day in crowded, smoky, dangerous factories, they went home to slums without windows or clean water or decent outhouses. Because they'd had little experience of cleanliness, poor people resisted the idea of washing. When a man was told that he needed to wash off his dirt, he protested that this would be like "robbing him of a great coat which he had had for some years."

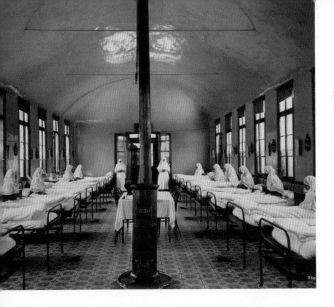

The Industrial Revolution spread most quickly in England, but the rest of Europe was not far behind. Between 1800 and 1850, industrial cities in Germany and France doubled in population. Filthy slums on both sides of the English Channel allowed diseases like typhus, diphtheria, and cholera to spread like wildfire.

Learning from the Indians

In 1858, Queen Victoria was crowned empress of India, although the British had ruled large parts of the country since the eighteenth century. Snobbishly, they felt superior to the Indians, but there was one thing that even the most prejudiced Englishman couldn't deny. At a time when the English were only starting to wash, Indians were much cleaner.

The British in India didn't wash their hair. They powdered it and put oils on it instead. But rats and cockroaches liked to snack on the powder and oils they found at the back of British heads. (Fun!) The Britons noticed that the Indians washed their own hair with boiled herbs and water, and that looked like a good idea. The word *shampoo* comes from the Hindi word *chompo*, meaning to press or massage.

The Public Bathhouse Returns

Something had to be done to make the slums less unhealthy, but repairing whole blocks and installing plumbing would take a long time. Building public baths, where poor people could bathe in private compartments, was quicker. Britain's first public bathhouse opened in Liverpool in 1842. Bathhouses soon opened in Hamburg and Berlin, and by the end of the century, almost every German city had at least one public bathhouse.

Unlike the English, Germans thought that the poor and the prosperous should bathe together—at least in the same building. Besides its lavish decorations, the Hohenstaufenbad, where Else and the Mesmers bathed, had three separate swimming pools (for middle-

Help! My Coat Is Drowning!

Before houses and apartments had bathrooms, which didn't happen until late in the nineteenth century in Europe, where to take a bath was a problem. Often the most convenient place to put a portable tub in a Parisian apartment was the hall. One day, in the dim light of a friend's hall, the painter Edouard Manet drowned his overcoat. After he had politely folded it and laid it down on what he thought was a lustrous, marble-topped table, the puzzled painter watched his coat sink: the table was a full tub!

and upper-class men, for middle- and upper-class women, and for workers of both sexes), a restaurant, a barbershop, and, depending on how much you paid, three different kinds of bathtubs—plain, nicer, and nicest.

Do you think you'd feel welcome in a fancy building where you had to enter at the back door? Right. Even though the motto of the German Association for People's Baths was "For every German, one bath a week," poor people stayed away from the bathhouses, and the average German took only five baths a year. The situation was pretty much the same in Britain and France. More men than women used the baths, partly because their work made them dirtier, they had fewer chores to do at home, and many women just did not want to take their clothes off in a public place, even a private bathing room.

Bathing in Green Soup

When the English writer and explorer Mary Kingsley traveled to West Africa in 1893, she described the baths taken by the M'pongwe and Igalwas people. Sometimes they bathed in tubs of hot water, but a favorite remedy for rheumatism involved bathing in a hole in the ground. Seven herbs, plus cardamom and peppers, were put into the hole. Boiling water was poured in, and the bather lowered herself into the soupy green mixture. After that, a framework of twigs was placed on top, then a layer of clay, leaving just the bather's head sticking out. There she stayed, for a few hours or as long as a day and a half. When she was taken out, her bath ended with a serious rubdown.

A nineteenth century M'pongwe woman

THE ABCs OF Washing

It was hard to convince grown-ups in France that, suddenly, dirt was not okay, so the experts decided to start with schoolchildren. Lessons about cleanliness showed up in every subject — not just in health and science classes, but also in dictation exercises, assigned reading, and recitations. A dictation for children in the early grades reads, "Louise does not like cold water. This morning, she thought she had washed herself because she gently passed the flannel across the end of her nose. Her face stayed dirty and her hands black. Her mother does not want to kiss her in that state."

"The Big Baths Killed Her Off"

The biggest problem with cleanliness in France was not city slums, but the country's large peasant population. Poor farmers still believed that dirt protected them, and some of their favorite sayings underlined the connection between cleanliness and danger, such as, "If you want to reach old age, don't take the oil off your skin."

Part of the problem was that the peasants associated washing with birth and death. If a peasant woman was bathed in a full-sized tub in a hospital or poorhouse, for example, and later died, people said, "It was the big baths that killed her off." No wonder people preferred staying dirty.

Chapter 6

Wet All Over at Once

NORTH AMERICA, 1800 TO 1900

Summer in Philadelphia

PHILADELPHIA, 1799

Rebecca, Jane, and Sarah thought Grandmother was being very silly. Grandfather had installed a shower in their backyard that summer, one of the first showers in town. The three girls loved getting into the tall box and pulling the chain that released the water stored in the overhead container.

You could hear their screams of laughter all up and down the street. Grandfather enjoyed the shower, too, but Grandmother refused to go in.

"It's not decent," she insisted. "Someone might see me entering or leaving."

"But, Grandmother," Rebecca, the eldest, said, "what is there to see? We all wear flannel gowns and oilcloth caps."

When Grandmother didn't have an answer for something, she usually changed the subject.

"It's not healthy to let water beat down on your head," she told the girls. "I'm sure it could make you ill, and it doesn't look very comfortable."

"It's better than comfortable, Grandmother," Rebecca said. "It's delightful."

"Hmmph," Grandmother said. But finally, the girls talked her into trying out the shower.

"We promise we won't let go of your hand," Rebecca said. "And we'll all go in together, so you'll be safe."

They waited until afternoon, so that the sun could warm the water in the container. Grandmother looked nervous, but Rebecca took one of her hands and Sarah the other. Rebecca hoisted little Jane up with her other arm. There was barely enough room for them in the shower, but they all managed to squeeze in.

"One, two, three!" counted Sarah. Then she pulled the chain, and warm water poured down. Grandmother gasped and squirmed at first, but finally she began to laugh, and the girls joined in.

That night at dinner, Grandmother spoke proudly about her adventure. "I bore it better than I expected," she told the girls' parents, "especially when I remember that I haven't been wet all over at once for 28 years."

America the Clean

At the start of the nineteenth century, Americans were as dirty as Europeans. But by the 1880s, something surprising had happened: this rough and ready land had become the Western country most devoted to cleanliness. By the end of the century, Americans, at least those who lived in cities, prided themselves on their cleanliness, compared with "filthy Europeans."

A Room and a Bath for a Dollar and a Half

Americans learned a lot about bathrooms from their hotels, which were designed for people who were willing to pay for luxuries. When Boston's Tremont House opened in 1829, the hotel world changed forever. Tremont House had individual locks on each of its 170 rooms and gaslight in the public rooms. Those were new ideas. But the newest thing of all was in the basement: eight bathing rooms where, as the hotel advertised, "guests could wash themselves all over."

Why did Americans take the lead when it came to cleanliness? One answer is because they could. It's much easier to install water and sewers in new cities than in old ones. With lots of cheap land available, people lived in houses that had space for bathrooms, unlike Europe's crowded apartments. Most people in North America had few or no servants; they would have to wash themselves so installing plumbing made sense. American plumbing was soon the best in the world.

While Europe loved the old and traditional, Americans loved what was new. Personal cleanliness was something new. Another reason they turned to cleanliness was the American belief in equality, eloquently expressed in the Declaration of Independence. No one in the United States of America could become a duke or princess or a member of the upper class by being born into it, so Americans looked for ways to distinguish themselves that were more fair. Cleanliness, which was possible for most Americans, turned out to be a good way to do that.

In 1836, something even more lavish opened—the Astor House in New York City. It had, amazingly, a bathroom and a toilet on each floor, supplied with water from a roof tank by a steam pump. After that, each fancy new hotel tried to top the Tremont and the Astor.

THE Story OF Soap PART THREE

During the sixteenth, seventeenth, and most of the eighteenth centuries, there was little or no demand for body soap in Europe. The rich women who used it, mostly on their face and hands, thought of soap more as a cosmetic or perfume than as a cleanser. Once Europeans had returned to using water, however, soap became an essential part of washing.

A few technical developments helped that change. A new process that produced soda ash from salt led to the development of a soap that was cheaper, harder, and milder than the gooey and irritating stuff made from wood ash. Animal fats, which came from goats, cattle, sheep, and—smelliest of all—whales and seals, produced yucky soap in shades of white, gray, and black. More efficient transportation made olive oil soaps from Spain and France more affordable, and soap manufacturers on both sides of the Atlantic experimented with formulas using cottonseed oil, coconut oil, and palm oil. Ivory and Palmolive soap (named for its blend of palm and olive oils) were early successes in the United States.

PART THREE

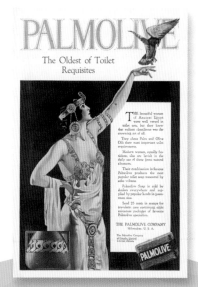

The War and Washing

You wouldn't expect that a long and bloody war would have much to do with washing, but the Civil War played a big part in American thinking about cleanliness. Even before the war began, Americans had been impressed with the work of the English nurse Florence

Nightingale during the Crimean War (1853–56). By scrubbing hospital walls and floors, laundering sheets and clothes, and washing patients, Nightingale revolutionized hospital conditions and saved many lives. She focused on the fact that deaths from disease and infection in wartime outnumbered those from gunshot wounds, and that cleanliness could reduce those deaths.

Inspired by her example, in the first year of the Civil War, the Union Army of the northern states founded an agency devoted to cleanliness for the army. Many people laughed at the idea, but the Sanitary Commission, as it was called, insisted that a man could not fight well unless he was clean. Each soldier was given a clothes brush, shoe brush, toothbrush, comb, and towel and was expected to use them. A 19-year-old soldier wrote home to Wisconsin complaining that staying clean took all his extra time!

The Sanitary Commission was successful. In the Mexican-American War of 1846–48, six soldiers died from disease for every one killed in battle. In the Union Army in the Civil War (1861–65), there were three deaths from disease to every two from gunshot wounds. Doctors and government officials had new respect for the power of cleanliness, and veterans returned home impressed with the comforts of hot water, foot baths, and toothbrushes. The average American in the northern states now connected cleanliness with progress, victory, and the American way of life.

Turning on the Taps

Plumbing was not unknown in the ancient world: the people of the Indus Valley civilization, Chinese, Persians, Aztecs, Greeks, and Romans devised ways of transporting, storing, and disposing of water. The best known of these systems, invented by the Romans, used aqueducts and lead pipes to deliver water to the imperial and neighborhood baths and to neighborhood wells. The surprising thing about the history of plumbing is that there were almost no developments beyond these rather basic services for almost 2,000 years, roughly from the beginning of the Common Era (CE) to the nineteenth century.

The growth of big cities, with fears about contaminated water, and renewed interest in cleanliness, finally spurred improvements. The Americans led the way, closely followed by England. The goal was pure hot and cold water delivered to every house and apartment, up to the topmost floor. Even in the United States, depending on where you lived, that might not be available until the 1920s, but the majority of houses did have running water by the end of the nineteenth century.

A modern water supply depends on high-pressure pumps, pipes, and a reservoir. Figuring that out began in the seventeenth century in Boston when wooden pipes carried water by gravity from a spring to a reservoir. Pumps, first run by steam power and then by water power, were gradually added.

The Gospel of the Toothbrush

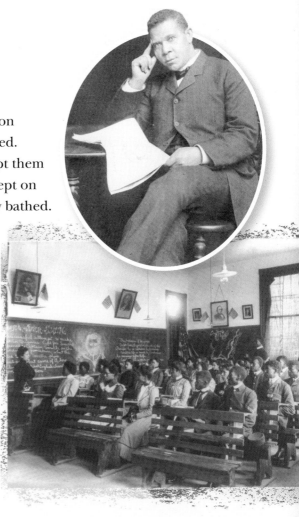

When the Civil War ended, four million African-American slaves had been freed. The slave owners had deliberately kept them so dependent that many had never slept on sheets, worn nightclothes, or formally bathed. For Booker T. Washington, the century's most famous African-American, cleanliness was key to independence. Born a slave, Washington had been taught neatness and cleanliness by a few strict but kind teachers. As a teenager, he walked and begged rides to a school 800 kilometers (500 miles) away that he longed to attend. When the head teacher asked him to sweep a classroom as part of his interview, Washington swept it three times and then dusted it four times. He was hired at the school as a janitor, which helped him to pay his tuition.

In 1881, Washington founded the Tuskegee Institute, a teachers' college in Alabama for African-Americans. He insisted on "absolute cleanliness of the body" and what he called "the gospel of the toothbrush." This idea became so well-known that students often arrived at Tuskegee carrying almost nothing but a toothbrush. Washington noticed that when a student replaced a worn-out toothbrush on her own, he could almost guarantee a good future for that person.

The Healing Powers of the Sweat Lodge

Native people from Mexico to Canada used versions of the sweat bath, and it was one of the first things travelers noticed. In 1665, David DeVries of New York admired how "entirely clean and more attractive than before" Native people looked after visiting a sweat lodge. The sweat lodge, usually a round, teepee-like structure heated by hot rocks or direct fire, was ideally built close to a river or lake, so the participants could jump in at the end. Not only did it clean the body, but Native people believed that it also had medicinal and spiritual powers. Cleaning and healing were fine according to American and Canadian government officials and missionaries, but they wanted to stamp out Native spirituality and convert the Native people to Christianity.

Nudists AND Butter-Stinkers

Europeans and Americans in the nineteenth century were pretty casual about cleanliness and scared to death about nakedness. Japan was the opposite—people there were obsessed with bathing and casual about nakedness. So when Westerners began traveling to Japan in the 1850s, both sides were amazed. The Japanese thought the foreigners smelled awful. Aside from the fact that Westerners didn't often wash, the Japanese traced the smell to their diet of meat and dairy—which the Japanese didn't eat—and called them "butter-stinkers." For their part, Westerners found the sight of naked Japanese people of both sexes bathing in a vat of hot water shocking. One day, some Western women were walking around a Tokyo garden when they came upon the gardener, who was having his bath outdoors in a tub. He was in water up to his shoulders, but when he saw the women, he jumped up, stood at attention, and bowed to them. Oh my goodness! The horrified ladies ran away in every direction.

In 1885, as part of their attempt to assimilate Native people, the Canadians prohibited sweat lodges, and two years later, the Americans followed suit. A seven-hour ceremony that involved building a teepee and heating rocks was not easy to hide! But the sweat lodge was so central to their way of life that many Native people did risk arrest by continuing to build them. The ban was not lifted until 1934 in the United States and 1951 in Canada.

The Newest Room in the House

At the beginning of the nineteenth century, most Americans bathed—those who did bathe—in a portable tub placed in the kitchen or bedroom. They spot-cleaned their hands, face, and other parts using a jug of water and a basin in their bedrooms, and when they needed a toilet, they went to the outhouse in the backyard. By the end of the century, many Americans, especially those living in the cities, did all those things in the newest room in the house: the bathroom.

At first, a bathroom was just that, a room with a fixed bathtub connected to plumbing. Early toilets were located in a separate, smaller room, and many people continued to use washbasins in their bedrooms until the end of the century. But by 1908, the Sears catalog offered Americans a choice of three complete "bathrooms" that included a tub, sink, and toilet. Depending on whether they were enameled steel or the more expensive enameled cast iron, the price ranged from $33.90 to $51.10.

Winter Wear

The hardest place to get and stay clean was on the frontier. Early in the twentieth century, an educated Englishwoman named Ella Sykes wrote a book about her experiences as a "home-help" in the western Canadian provinces. The only washing she saw was done at an enamel basin in the kitchen, where the farmworkers cleaned their hands and faces and dried them on a grimy towel. A schoolteacher in Alberta told Sykes that when she tried to replace the top button on an immigrant boy's shirt, she discovered that the child's mother had sewn him into it for the winter.

Americanizing THE Newcomers

In the 1880s, hundreds of thousands of Southern and Eastern Europeans began arriving in the United States. By 1900, 37 percent of New York City's three and a half million people were immigrants. How to Americanize these foreigners? By preaching cleanliness. Schools were the place where it was enforced most intensely. Teachers taught children the use of the washbowl and soap. They inspected students for dirt and sent them home if they found too much of it. In one New York City school, the principal ordered the teachers to ask the children every day, "What must I do to be healthy?"

The children had to answer in unison:

> I must keep my skin clean
>
> Wear clean clothes
>
> Breathe pure air
>
> And live in the sunlight.

But empty resolutions didn't do any good: what these immigrant kids needed to make them clean and healthy was running water and well-ventilated apartments.

Chapter 7

Soap Opera

1875 TO 1960

It's Only an Ad

TORONTO, 1933

Charlie was in trouble, and his parents had sent him to his room.

It began because he wanted his father to go outside and play catch with him. He never seemed to have time to play with Charlie. His father was listening to the radio. Someone with a deep voice was talking about a man who didn't get the job he wanted because he hadn't looked clean enough. If only he had bathed with Palmolive, things would have turned out much more successfully . . .

Oh, it's an ad, Charlie thought, and lost interest.

"Dad? Please? Can we go outside now?"

"Just a minute. I want to hear this."

"Why? It's just an ad."

His father scowled. "Ads give us information that's interesting and helpful, Charlie. I said we'd go in a minute."

Charlie stalked off, scuffing his feet against the living room carpet. His mother sat reading a magazine at the dining room table. Charlie noticed that she-had stopped at an advertisement for Lux soap that showed a young bride. The caption underneath the picture read, "Skin That Says 'I Do!'"

His mother said, as if she were thinking out loud, "There's a special offer for Lux coming up at the drugstore this week."

Now it was Charlie's turn to scowl.

"A soap isn't going to make you look like that bride," he said grumpily. "And why do you care? You're already married. They just want to sell you their product, and you're falling for their line."

Charlie's father appeared in the doorway.

"That's enough, Charlie! You were rude to me, but I won't have you being rude to your mother. Now go to your room and stay there until you understand how to behave."

There was nothing to do in Charlie's room, which he supposed was part of his punishment. Finally, under a stack of games, he found a magazine. He paged through it, skipping the boring love stories and pictures of dresses. He stopped at a drawing of a friendly looking boy sitting in a bathtub. The boy was in a splashing contest with his father, who held a towel ready for him. Charlie liked the teasing expression on the boy's face, and the father looked nice too, as if he were having fun.

The caption under the picture read, "Strong bodies crave this." What was "this"? Lifebuoy soap, Charlie read. Oh, it was only an ad. He started to turn the page, but the picture of the boy and his father told a story, and Charlie liked it despite himself. He wanted to have more fun with his father. Could using Lifebuoy really make that happen? For the first time, an ad had worked its magic on skeptical Charlie.

"It floats!"

Procter & Gamble was good at making household cleaners and laundry detergent, but the Ohio company had been trying for years to create a soap gentle enough for skin. Finally, in 1878, they had a winning recipe. They planned to call it P&G White Soap . . . at least they did until Harley Procter, the company's sales manager, heard that idea. "Boring!" he said, which meant it became his job to think up a better name. One Sunday in church, while the minister was reading a psalm, a line—something about ivory palaces—caught Procter's attention. Ivory, he thought: it suggested something strong and beautiful. Inspired, he christened the hard white soap Ivory.

A year later, Procter & Gamble had another piece of luck. A worker left the new soap's steam-powered mixing machine unattended for too long. Everyone assumed that the overflowing lather in the vat would be useless, but when it hardened and was cut into cakes, not only did it still clean, it floated. That gave rise to Ivory's long-lived motto, "It floats!" Adding another slogan, "99 $\frac{44}{100}$% pure," Ivory promised customers an airy, immaculate product.

The Sweet Smell of Success

When it came to understanding the importance of catchy names and slogans, Harley Procter was ahead of his time, but soap makers and advertisers were natural allies. In fact, toilet soap and advertising grew up together. Both had been around in some form for centuries, but they only became large-scale businesses in the late 1800s.

As advertising took its place in the modern world, it tried out new gimmicks on toilet soap. Celebrities, such as actresses and singers, were hired to claim that a particular soap made their skin glow or enhanced their beauty. Soap companies offered small "gifts" to customers who sent in a certain number of soap wrappers. Sapolio Soap ran a series of ads about a jolly place called "Spotless Town," whose people spoke in simple, memorable jingles. All these techniques—testimonials, prizes, catchy slogans and jingles, and appealing characters—were later used in ad campaigns for all kinds of products, but they first appeared in advertisements for soap. Advertisers started to aim their products at different audiences as well—for example, the romantic daytime radio serials written for women always featured ads for soap. As a result, these shows became known as "soap operas," and later "soaps".

The ads' messages worked, especially in North America. As cities grew, more people got jobs in offices and factories, and they started to notice the smells produced by their bodies and those of others. As more women entered the work world, people worried more about "offending" others by not being clean or odorless enough. ("Offending" was one of soap advertisers' favorite words.)

No-see-ums

When a Viennese doctor named Ignaz Semmelweis proposed in the mid-1800s that delivery room doctors and medical students wash their hands before dealing with patients, people ridiculed his idea. It wasn't until the early twentieth century that the germ theory—the belief that many diseases are caused by organisms too small to be seen except through a microscope—won approval from doctors and public health experts. It was a huge breakthrough, but also scary. Until antibiotics were invented in the 1930s and 1940s, almost the only way to fight germs was to wash them off. Manufacturers on both sides of the Atlantic worked even harder to come up with a soap that was gentler on the skin and affordable for the average person.

Some Things Are So Good They Don't Need Advertising

The people of Zimbabwe, in southern Africa, had a traditional practice called "smearing." After they washed, they rubbed a mixture of oil or fat and earth on their bodies. That protected them from harmful dirt and other threats to their health, kept their skin from drying out, and gave their bodies a glamorous shine.

When Western soaps came to Zimbabwe in the twentieth century, the ads concentrated on power and beauty. African men were supposed to buy Lifebuoy, a strong soap with carbolic disinfectant, because "The successful man uses Lifebuoy." Women were supposed to buy Lux because "Africa's loveliest women use Lux beauty soap."

But Zimbabweans didn't feel really clean without coating themselves in a rich, silky paste, and the custom of smearing has never died out. Instead of mixing oil and earth, people began looking for commercial products that would protect their skin and make it shine—things like margarine, cooking oil, and even the oil from the top of the peanut butter jar! By a process of trial and error, Zimbabweans finally decided that the best things for smearing after washing were Vaseline or cold cream, which are widely used today. First they wash with the soaps they see in ads; then they smear with the products they found for themselves—that advertising had nothing to do with.

Always a Bridesmaid, Never a Bride

In the 1920s, prosperity in North America was at an all-time high. That meant people could afford lots of products. And—surprise—every time advertisers introduced a new problem, they offered a product that would solve it.

Listerine is a good example of advertisers' ability to create a "need." Invented as a surgical antiseptic, Listerine turned out to be tremendously versatile. Without changing the recipe, its owners, Lambert Pharmacal, began marketing Listerine to dentists as an oral antiseptic and then to the general public as a mouthwash. But sales weren't great, so the company's president, Gerard Lambert, asked the company chemist to catalog Listerine's uses. There was one word in the list that Lambert didn't understand: "halitosis". When the chemist explained that it meant bad breath, a new identity for a middle-aged product was born.

People had noticed bad breath at least since the time of the ancient Greeks. And everybody knew about romances

A SAFE ANTISEPTIC

—to prevent infection of cuts and wounds

—to keep teeth sound, and for mouth cleanliness

—as a lotion after shaving

LISTERINE

that didn't work out and job offers and promotions that never came. The reason behind many of these everyday heartbreaks, Lambert Pharmacal assured people in a series of irresistible ads, was smelly breath.

Take Edna, a pretty girl who was "often a bridesmaid but never a bride." Or Smedley, a man who looked attractive to women until they caught a whiff of his breath. An ad titled, "Are you unpopular with

Camels in the Caldarium

In 1937, the Italian dictator Benito Mussolini initiated outdoor operas at the Baths of Caracalla for families who couldn't afford to leave Rome in the summer. The ruins of the hot room, which included 30-meter- (100-foot-) high pillars from the original bath, were so huge that a stage 30 meters (100 feet) long and 50 meters (162 feet) wide was built. It was perfect for productions of Verdi's opera *Aida*, which featured at various times camels, elephants, horses, lions, and chariots, as well as the cast. Operas and other musical events are still performed in the hot room every summer.

your own children?" showed a frowning little boy trying to escape his mother's hug. The most worrying thing (and the most moneymaking claim for Listerine's makers) was that no one was likely to tell you that you had halitosis, and you couldn't discover it for yourself. Plus, according to the ads, bad breath was a nationwide epidemic!

Gargling with Listerine became a morning routine for millions of North Americans, and Lambert's annual profits rose from $115,000 in 1921 to more than $8 million in 1928. No one ever duplicated the extent of Listerine's success, but it showed advertisers how much money could be made by worrying people about the way they smelled.

THE Continental Divide

By the 1930s, almost all houses and apartments in North American cities had hot water plumbing, and so did a smaller majority in Britain. But only 10 percent of Italians had a bathroom at the time. In France in the 1950s, only one house or apartment in 10 had a shower or bath.

Every time the Americans went a step further down the road to "perfect" cleanliness—deciding that people should bathe or shower and put on deodorant every day, or that women should shave their underarms to limit body odor— Europeans scoffed. To them, these ideas seemed silly, or impossible, or both.

Odor? Oh, No!

On a hot day in 1907, a Cincinnati doctor named A. D. Murphey noticed that he was sweating while doing surgery. He invented a deodorant for himself based on aluminum chloride. He had no interest in marketing his idea, but his teenaged daughter, Edna, did. She named the deodorant Odorono (for "Odor? Oh, no!"), borrowed $150 from her grandfather, and began manufacturing and marketing it.

She also enlisted an ad writer, James Webb Young, who wrote one of the most sensational ads in the twentieth century for *The Ladies' Home Journal.* An illustration showed an attractive couple, with the woman extending her arm up to the man's shoulder. The headline was, "Within the Curve of a Woman's Arm," and the subtitle promised a "frank discussion of a subject too often avoided." The ad spoke plainly about the active perspiration glands under a person's arm, and included the familiar, scary warning about odors that may be "unnoticed by ourselves, but distinctly noticeable to others."

The public wasn't used to reading about women and sweat, and several women who knew the ad writer threatened never to speak to him again. Two hundred readers of *The Ladies' Home Journal* canceled their subscriptions in protest. But sales for Odorono rose 112 percent within a year of the ad's appearance.

Always Ready to Be Cleaner

Sales boomed in the 1920s for soap, shampoo, and deodorants, but manufacturers of those products were worried. Paved streets, cars, and electricity kept people cleaner than had the old dirt roads, horses, coal stoves, and kerosene lamps. Better central heating meant people didn't have to wear heavy woolen clothes inside, so they sweated less. Mechanized factories and labor-saving devices soiled workers and housewives less, too.

But while sales of personal hygiene products did slow in the 1930s during the Great Depression, they soon climbed back. Americans had a genius for advertising and a bottomless wish to be cleaner: this meant that they led the world in successful campaigns for grooming products. Millions of Americans still feared smelly mouths, underarms, and feet, and the most famous movie stars of the day recommended soap ("9 out of 10 Screen Stars are Lux Girls") as the way to lovelier skin.

Keeping Clean in a Poor Country

In mid-twentieth-century China, the only way for most people to wash was with a simple enamel basin. Some people had a stand on which they set the basin; others put it on a counter or a table. You filled the basin with hot water from a thermos, and then dipped your towel in the water to wipe your body.

In the Chinese countryside, people traditionally cleaned their teeth with salt, using a willow stick that had been frayed at one end. But by the 1930s, if you lived in the eastern city of Hangzhou, you had a choice of more than 78 different styles of modern toothbrushes and dozens of toothpastes. Because money was scarce, the toothpaste came with a key so you could press out the last little bit.

Chapter 8

The Household Shrine

1960 TO THE PRESENT

The Secrets of the Charm Box

SEATTLE, 1985

"Molly? You're next," Mr. Warren said.

Feeling nervous, Molly took her notes to the front of the classroom. Unlike the other kids, she didn't put any pictures or illustrations on the easel. The assignment was to present a different society to the class. So far, her classmates had described the Zuni in Arizona, the Innu in Labrador, and the Sami in Sweden.

Molly took a deep breath and began.

"My presentation is about a group of people who haven't been studied very much. They are the Nacirema, and they live in North America."

"Where in North America do they live?" a boy waving his hand asked.

Gulp, first problem. Molly thought fast.

"If you don't mind, I'll take questions at the end."

Mr. Warren nodded and she went on.

"The Nacirema are quite rich, but they think they're ugly and they worry a lot about getting sick. So they build a very special place in their houses: a household shrine. They go there often, performing special actions they hope will improve their lives."

The class looked puzzled as Molly continued.

"The most powerful people have several shrines in their houses," she explained. "Every shrine has a charm box on the wall that's full of powders and potions for adults and children. Underneath the box, there's a basin for holy water that gets used in different rituals. In one ritual, people even put a brush made of pig hair into their mouths and move it around. Kids have to do it too."

"Eww! Putting pig hair in your mouth!" Robbie cried.

"That is too gross!" David pretended to vomit.

"That's not all," said Molly. "Although these practices are very important to them, the Nacirema don't do them together, like in other societies. They are all done privately."

As soon as Molly finished her presentation, hands shot up with questions. But instead of answering them, Molly posed a question of her own.

"Do the Nacirema sound at all familiar?" she asked her classmates.

Hands went down, and people's faces looked blank.

"Did you notice anything about their name?" Molly hinted.

More blank faces.

So she had to tell them.

"Nacirema," she said, "is *American* spelled backward."

Finally they got it, and people began to laugh. The "household shrine" was nothing more than a bathroom! The charm box was a medicine cabinet! Molly explained that an anthropologist named Horace Miner had invented the Nacirema to make fun of the American obsession with appearance, health, and cleanliness.

"Very clever, Molly," Mr. Warren said. "I was wondering why you hadn't made any drawings to go with your presentation."

"Yes," she said, smiling. "It's pretty hard to make a sink and a medicine cabinet look mysterious."

The More the Merrier, the Bigger the Better

Horace Miner published his mock-serious spoof, "Body Ritual Among the Nacirema," in 1956. If he were writing it today, he would have to make the household shrine he describes even more exaggerated, and people's rituals and potions more complicated.

Miner pointed out that the Nacirema judged people's wealth by the number of bathrooms they had. Since then, bathrooms have multiplied even more. In the luxury apartments in the Stanhope Hotel on Fifth Avenue in New York City, an eight-bedroom apartment features eleven bathrooms (with two for the master bedroom). The bathrooms could outnumber the residents!

Almost one in four houses built in the United States in 2005 has three or more bathrooms. Not only are there more of them, bathrooms today are bigger. The average size of the American bathroom tripled between 1994 and 2004.

Turning Their Backs on the Household Shrine

Cleanliness was so central to North American life that when young women and men in the 1960s wanted to rebel against their parents, teachers, and other authorities, giving up deodorant, haircuts, shaving, and regular

washing was an obvious way to go. Long hair, handmade clothes, peace symbols, bare feet, and biblical beards showed that you were against advertising, business, and war. These folks, called hippies, attracted lots of disapproval because their appearance, their politics, and their attitude to life challenged the values of the day. In 1966, one authority figure, then-governor of California Ronald Reagan, defined a hippie as someone who "dresses like Tarzan, has hair like Jane, and smells like Cheetah."

Bring Back THE Bucket

The traditional way to wash in India was with a bucket and a pitcher. When running water came to the cities—in many places not until the late twentieth century—Indians celebrated. Except, that is, in the heat of summer. In New Delhi, for example, water is often available only for a few hours once or twice a day, and people save that water in an overhead tank. In summer, the water in the tank gets hideously hot—and a hot shower is not fun when the temperature outside is 38 degrees Celsius (100 degrees Fahrenheit) and higher! So during the summer season, many Indians return to the bucket and pitcher. They store water overnight in buckets, and in the morning, they pour the cold water over themselves. It saves water, and it's like standing under a small waterfall. Cool!

High-Tech, or Never-Never Land?

Today, luxury bathrooms look more and more like science fiction. Oversized tubs fill in 60 seconds, bathroom scales calculate muscle/ fat ratios, faucets with infrared sensors spout water without being touched. Mirrors are fogless, plasma TV screens are waterproof, and showers imitate rain-forest downpours.

If you're rich, you can also turn your bathroom into a faraway place. Maybe you'd like a Japanese-style "wet room," where the shower isn't in a cubicle but sprays the whole room. Or you'd rather travel to the past, perhaps to Rome. If your floor can support it, an 820-kilogram (1,800-pound) marble tub with claw feet could be just the imperial make-believe for you. Or, if you like the idea of sociable medieval steam baths, you could get a bathtub built for four people.

"I'll Take a Navy Shower"

The average North American uses about 375 liters (100 gallons) of water a day, compared to 190 liters (50 gallons) per person in France and 7.5 to 19 liters (2 to 5 gallons) in sub-Saharan Africa. Before you scorn North Americans as water gluttons, think back to the ancient Romans. With their super-efficient aqueducts and extravagant bathhouses, the average Roman had 1,135 liters (300 gallons) of water a day at his or her disposal!

Still, dry conditions in California, Texas, Florida, and other places across North America are undeniable and worrying. Many experts think that climate change will make major droughts more likely in the future. In 2015, when a serious drought in California was in its fourth year, the governor of the state reduced water use by 25 percent, except for agriculture.

Although most of the water Californians need to stop wasting is used for watering lawns, not bodies, it still takes a lot of water to be clean. The average US shower lasts 8 minutes and uses 65 liters (17.2 gallons), while the average bath can take 132 liters to 190 liters (35 to 50 gallons). We're throwing an awful lot of water over ourselves to clean off a few specks of dirt. Water in North America is very cheap— we pay less than half what Europeans do for their water—and there's nothing like money to make people more careful. Some people think charging more for water would be a way to start conserving it.

Here are a few ideas you can try yourself to save water:

1. Suggest that your parents install a low-flow showerhead and a timer on the shower so that it stops at a set time.

2. Take a "navy shower" (named for life on a ship, where water is scarce) by turning off the water while you soap and shampoo, then turning it back on for the rinse. You can do the same while washing your hands and brushing your teeth.

The Toilet That Washes

Japanese toilets are the most versatile in the world. They can greet the user, warm his or her seat, deodorize the room, and measure blood sugar, pulse, and blood pressure. But most important for the Japanese, their toilets WASH — which is why they call them washlets. Depending on which buttons you press, a water jet cleaner and a blow dryer will clean your rear end and your private parts — all while you're sitting on the toilet. Excuse me, the washlet.

3. Put a bucket under the tap while the shower water warms up, and use the cold water for plants.

4. Shower less often. Give your dirty parts a stand-up wash with soap and a wet facecloth instead.

The No-Poo People

Today, a small but vocal movement of people are taking a new approach to clean. They shower and bathe much less and spot-clean more often. To stop their armpits from smelling, they rub a slice of lemon on them. Some stop washing their hair for as long as six months, calling their anti-shampoo movement No-Poo.

Some of these people are concerned about the environment: they want to save water and avoid pouring toxic creams, lotions, soaps, and

Shampooing IN THE New Year

People in North America and Europe celebrate New Year's Eve by partying and drinking champagne. In Java, they celebrate it by washing their hair! On May 7, which is the eve of the new year in the Islamic and Javanese calendars, people travel to holy places all over Java so they can shampoo themselves in rivers, springs, and special pools around midnight—often in the company of thousands of other shampooers. In addition to New Year's, the Javanese reach for their shampoo to mark other transitions—when a girl starts to menstruate, after a birth or a death, before a marriage, and before fasting for the month of Ramadan begins.

shampoos down the drain into our lakes and rivers. Some are tired of advertisers controlling our behavior and our spending. The No-Poo people claim their hair is much shinier and healthier now that they aren't drying it out with shampoo. And, finally, more and more people are starting to think that washing our bodies removes bacteria that we need. (See more on that in the next chapter).

No One Leaves This Sauna Until We Agree!

Finland has more saunas than cars — there are 5.3 million people in Finland, and 3 million saunas. Almost all Finns take their first sauna by the age of two, and 99 percent of grown-ups take at least one sauna a week (which can take about two and a half hours). A popular TV show that ran for years centered on two male hosts who invited famous people to take off their clothes and share a sauna — male people, since women and men don't normally take saunas together. Guests included a dozen cabinet ministers and more than a hundred members of parliament.

The Finnish parliament has its own sauna, and, until recently, when government leaders couldn't agree on an issue, they continued their discussion there. Every Finnish embassy around the world had a sauna, and diplomats practiced "sauna diplomacy," where they invited (read: politely insisted) the parties in a disagreement to steam away their differences. Things began to change in the twenty-first century, as more and more women entered political life in Finland. Forty percent of members of Parliament are women, and a woman, Tarja Halonen, was president of Finland from 2000 to 2012. Women leaders do meet in the sauna, but some of them say it takes too long!

Chapter 9

Good Microbes, Bad Microbes

INTO THE FUTURE

Invisible Friends

PORTLAND, MAINE, 2015

Kyle was worried. The science fair was only a few weeks away, and he hadn't come up with a project yet. His friends spent the lunch hour talking about their cool ideas—building a rainwater collection system, designing an experiment to test whether smiling was contagious, inventing a battery that would clean silver. He'd racked his brains, but he still hadn't thought of anything. He was in the kitchen making popcorn when he heard his mom calling him from the living room.

"Kyle, come and check out this TV program. It's about something called the human microbiome, and it's fascinating."

"Never heard of it," Kyle called back grumpily. He had nothing better to do, though, so he reluctantly joined his mom on the couch.

His mother had muted the TV while the commercials were on. "This show says we're covered with trillions of invisible microorganisms that live on our skin and inside our bodies," she explained to Kyle, bouncing on the coach a little as she did so. His mom was always getting excited about this kind of thing. "Apparently, they outnumber our body cells by ten to one. They're bacteria mostly, but also fungi and viruses. Scientists used to think these creatures were bad for us, but now they're learning that our microbiome also helps us in really important ways."

The commercials finished, and Kyle's mother clicked off the mute button. Kyle was only planning to watch the show for a few minutes, to make his mom happy, but he was hooked right away. The microbiome really *was* fascinating. It helped people to make their own vitamins, digest food, and keep their immune systems strong, he learned. Human microbiomes were so individual that an artist had even created a weird gallery of "portraits" by culturing the microbes in different people's belly buttons!

Some of the stuff on the program was downright gross. For example, Kyle learned that some doctors had started inserting poop from one person's body into another's to cure a dangerous infection called *C. difficile.* And the scientists on the show talked a lot about how people's obsession with being clean was actually harming them. Kyle liked that, too.

After a short segment about how kids who live with pets are less likely to have allergies, asthma, and other health problems, Kyle suddenly jumped up. "That's it!" he yelled.

His mother looked startled. "*What's* it?" she asked.

"My project! I'll do an experiment that separates kids into two groups, some who have pets and some who don't. I can swab their hands and run the swab in an agar plate, incubate the plates in the dark for 24 hours, and then compare them. Like that scientist said, the plates of the kids with pets should show a much bigger range of microbes than the other ones do. Wow. This is going to be the coolest science project of all!"

The Rise of the Mysophobe

A mysophobe is a person with an extreme fear of germs and dirt. These days, mysophobes can seem almost normal. The recent outbreaks and epidemics of bird flu, SARS, *E. coli*, Norwalk virus, MRSA, and Ebola have made people want to run for cover.

Until the 1990s, antibacterial soaps were seen mostly in doctors' offices and hospitals, but since then, many antibacterial products for the general public have hit the drugstore shelves. They don't clean any better than plain soap and water, though, and using so many of these products can make us resistant to antibiotics when we really need them.

Antibacterials are only the start. Some people these days avoid shaking hands; if they must do so, they wash their hands or use sanitizer afterward as soon as they can. You can buy a portable strap to use on the subway, so that your hands never have to touch the overhead bar, as well as a strip of vinyl that covers your supermarket cart handle. You can store your toothbrush in a holder that kills germs with ultraviolet light.

Public bathrooms are especially scary to many people. One solution is a plastic box installed above the doorknob or door-pull in a public toilet that sprays a disinfectant mist every 15, 30, or 60 minutes. Or how about the SanitGrasp, a U-shaped gadget that replaces door handles and knobs in public places, allowing the door to be opened with your forearm? Manufacturers are coming up with more and more of these products—which make people more scared than ever.

Don't Touch That Handle

Missy Cohen-Fyffe, a New Hampshire mother, didn't want her baby son holding "the germy metal handle" of the carts in the supermarket. To solve that problem, she sewed him a cotton liner that had holes for his legs but covered the handle. Every time she went shopping, people asked her where they could buy the liner, so she founded a company, Babe Ease. Its products include the shopping cart liner, a cover to prevent contact with "grimy wooden restaurant high-chairs," and a cover for diaper-changing areas. Business is brisk, with the big box stores now selling Babe Ease products.

Better Safe Than Sick

According to two Toronto emergency room doctors, some simple practices could prevent you from getting sick in the next epidemic or pandemic. Get a flu shot by all means, they say. Be careful around live birds and eat only well-cooked chicken and turkey. During a pandemic or even a normal flu outbreak, wash your hands often, and cover your face when you sneeze or cough. Stay at least one meter (three feet) away from sick people; if you're caring for someone sick, wear gloves and a mask. Suggest to your family that you keep some rubber gloves and containers of hand sanitizer with your emergency supplies.

Are Microbes our friends?

But while some people strive to make their lives as bacteria-free as possible, scientists are now moving in the opposite direction. By the end of the twentieth century, doctors were noticing a steep rise in allergies and asthma among North American and European kids. A British scientist named D. P. Strachan made a shocking suggestion about the cause. Strachan's idea, which he called the Hygiene Hypothesis, was that our immune systems need a certain amount of bacteria on which to flex their muscles. Without that, the white cells designed to fight bacteria in our bodies, called Th1 lymphocytes, don't develop, and Th2 lymphocytes—white cells whose job it is to defend us against germs—develop too much. Without the check and balance of well-exercised Th1 lymphocytes, the Th2 system overreacts, and the immune system produces allergies. To Strachan, it looked as if the extreme cleanliness of prosperous countries was bad for our health.

In the late 1980s, a German doctor, Erika von Mutius, compared allergies and asthma in children from East Berlin and West Berlin. She expected to find that kids living in poor and polluted East Berlin would have higher rates than the children from clean, prosperous West Berlin. She found just the opposite: the kids in West Berlin had more asthma and a greater number of allergic reactions.

The research that followed began to fill in a fascinating picture. Kids who had lots of brothers and sisters (especially older siblings and especially brothers, generally dirtier than sisters), lived on a farm, had a cat, or who went to day care in their first year turned out to be best at avoiding allergic diseases. The kids most likely to develop allergies and asthma were only children who lived in cities, did not attend day care, had no pets, washed their hands more than five times a day, and bathed more than once a day. (Tell *that* one to your parents!)

The Hygiene Hypothesis is still just a hypothesis (an idea or thesis that has not yet been proven), but many scientists take it seriously. There is some contrary evidence—dust mites and cockroaches have been connected with the development of asthma—and we can't all surround ourselves with animals or move to a farm. A good place to start, however, would be to end our war-on-germs thinking. Tore Midtvedt, a Swedish expert on microbes, explains, "I'm not saying we should be more dirty. I'm saying we should be less clean." In other words, we could loosen our strict standards a lot before getting to a dangerously dirty state.

One Sure Thing

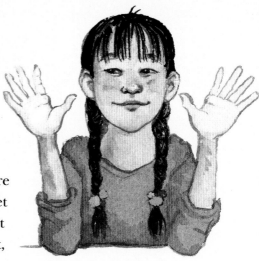

Most of the 100 trillion microbes we carry around inside our bodies and on our skin are good for us— helping us to digest our food and to battle disease and stress—but some are harmful. How can we make sure we let the good ones do their thing but fight the bad ones? The best way to do that, it turns out, is by washing our hands. In fact, unless you play contact sports or do farmwork, you wouldn't harm your health if you NEVER washed above your wrists.

Hand-washing doesn't sound very dramatic. It's a simple practice that has been around forever. Telemachus and his family in *The Odyssey* washed their hands before they prayed and ate. Medieval knights and ladies washed their hands before eating, and even Louis XIV, the seventeenth-century French king who rarely washed any other part of himself, started each day with clean hands. Today, the Centers for Disease Control and Prevention in the United States call hand-washing vitally important and "a do-it-yourself vaccine."

Human and animal poop contain germs such as *E. coli*, salmonella, and norovirus that cause food poisoning. Feces also can spread respiratory illnesses like pneumonia. Using the toilet or changing a diaper can get those germs on your hands, and from there into your mouth. So can handling raw meat with invisible animal poop on it. Remember, one gram (a fraction of an ounce) of human poop— about the weight of a paper clip—contains one trillion germs! Each year, about 2.2 million children under five die of diarrheal illnesses and pneumonia. Washing hands with soap could prevent a third of childhood cases of diarrhea worldwide and one out of six cases of childhood pneumonia. That's pretty impressive for 20 seconds of rubbing with soap and water!

The Dirt on Clean

Cleanliness in the twenty-first century is a tangle of contradictions. Some people buy antibacterial ballpoint pens, germ-free calculators, and workout clothes embedded with antimicrobial agents—silver, carbon, or ceramic bonded into the fabric—to prevent bacteria from multiplying. Other people argue that we need to live in less-than-laboratory-clean conditions for the sake of our health. At the same time, there are large parts of the world where people would love to have the sanitary conditions that most North Americans have.

Two Cheers for Not-So-Clean

Dishes washed in dishwashers have less bacteria than dishes washed by hand. So dishwashers are good, right? Not so fast. A study done of Swedish kids aged seven and eight found that kids who ate from hand-washed dishes—that is, dishes with more invisible creepy-crawlies on them—were less likely to get eczema, asthma, and hay fever than kids who ate from dishes washed by a machine.

Sucking on your baby sister's pacifier and putting it back in her mouth is gross, right? Not necessarily so. Swedish babies whose parent licked a dirty pacifier before popping it back into the baby's mouth had lower rates of eczema and asthma than babies whose parents washed the pacifier with water.

These two studies suggest there is truth to the Hygiene Hypothesis. One mother of a two-year-old who washes his pacifier with water said she didn't think the study would make her start sucking it. "But sometimes the dog cleans it off for us," she added, "so maybe that's just as good." Eww!

Hand-Washing 101

FROM THE CENTERS FOR DISEASE CONTROL AND PREVENTION

Happy birthday to yoouuu

1. Wet your hands with clean, running water (warm or cold), turn off the tap (to save water), and apply soap.

2. Lather your hands by rubbing them together with the soap. Be sure to lather the backs of your hands, between your fingers, and under your nails. [Microbes especially love to be under your nails.]

3. Scrub for at least 20 seconds, the time it would take to sing "Happy Birthday" twice or "Yankee Doodle Dandy" once.

4. Rinse your hands well under clean, running water.

5. Dry your hands using a clean towel or air-dry them. [Why? Because germs move more easily to and from wet hands.]

Probably differing views on cleanliness were always like this. The ancient Greeks argued about cold- and hot-water bathing. French peasants thought water was dangerous while teachers tried to convince them it was healthy. The Muslims in Spain washed regularly, so the Spaniards stayed dirty, to show they were Christians. Later, the dirty Spaniards mystified the clean Aztecs. Cleanliness has never been straightforward.

Middle-class North Americans, sitting all day in front of their computers, with houses full of labor-saving appliances, have never

New Life for Old Bathhouses

France's public bathhouses were built at a time when bathrooms were rare in apartments. When modern plumbing became widespread, most of the baths were converted to other uses or demolished. But in the twenty-first century, a downturn in the economy and a change in immigration patterns have made the surviving baths newly popular, especially in poorer neighborhoods. In the working-class sections of Paris, mostly in the northeast of the city, attendance has tripled since 2000, with around 900,000 admissions every year. The situation is similar in the French city of Lille, where there are too few baths to accommodate the immigrants who use them regularly, including many Roma families from Eastern Europe. In Lyon, mostly homeless people patronized the baths in the recent past, but now they are used by the working poor, construction workers, students, and an increasing influx of Albanian and Bulgarian refugees.

needed to wash less, and have never scrubbed more thoroughly. Rather than smell like human beings, we spend billions of dollars every year on soaps, sanitizers, gels, creams, and lotions that make us smell like tea, or tropical fruit, or cookies. Our ancestors would be astonished.

The future of cleanliness is a mystery. But one thing seems certain: a century from now, when people with their own ideas look back at what we consider "clean," they will be amused—if not amazed.

Image Credits

Front cover: tub, mirror, chair, wallpaper, © iStock.com/AlexandrMoroz, ceramic tiles, © Robertds/Dreamstime.com, steam, © Denitsa Glavinova/Dreamstime; 3, 35, © Palex66/Dreamstime.com; 9, © iStock.com/Linda Steward; 10, © Maurie Hill/Dreamstime.com; 11, Wellcome Library, London: http://creativecommons.org/licenses/by/4.0/; 12, Science Museum, London, Wellcome Images: http://creativecommons.org/licenses/by/4.0/: note: original image close-cropped; 15 top, © iStock.com/Bruno_il_segretario; 15 bottom, © Iakov Filimonov/Dreamstime.com; 17, Wellcome Library, London: http://creativecommons.org/licenses/by/4.0/: note: original image close-cropped; 18, © Atosan/Dreamstime.com; 19, Gift of Jo and Howard Weiner, courtesy The Museum of Photographic Arts; 22, Wellcome Library, London: http://creativecommons.org/licenses/by/4.0/: note: original image slightly cropped; 23, © iStock.com/wahahaz; 25, © iStock.com/Jasmina Mihoc; 26 top, © Bufka/Dreamstime.com; 26 bottom, © Thedreamstock/Dreamstime.com; 27, © iStock.com/nicoolay; 28, Library of Congress, Reproduction Number: LC-USZ62-95240; 31, © Muslianshah Masrie/Alamy Stock Photo; 33 (cropped), © INTERFOTO/Alamy Stock Photo; 33 frame, 41 frame, 43 frame, 47 bottom frame, gillmar/Shutterstock.com; 36, © iStock.com/duncan1890; 37 top, © Walker Art Library/Alamy Stock Photo; 37 bottom, Library of Congress, Reproduction Number: LC-USZC4-8455; 39, © iStock.com/AxPitel; 40, © Ann Moore/Dreamstime.com; 41 (cropped), © Heritage Image Partnership Ltd/Alamy Stock Photo; 43, Clipart.com; 44, Library of Congress, Reproduction Number: LC-DIG-ggbain-19518; 45, © iStock.com/HultonArchive; 46, © iStock.com/alrikki; 47 top, © iStock.com/duncan1890; 47 bottom (cropped), © Peter Horree/Alamy Stock Photo; 49, Library of Congress, Reproduction Number: LC-USZC2-3582; 50, © Ken Backer/Dreamstime.com; 51, © Horacio Villalobos/Corbis; 53, Picture: CARASANA; 54, © iStock.com/duncan1890; 55, photo by Charles Marville, gift Government of France, 1881: courtesy State Library of Victoria; 56, Library of Congress, Reproduction Number: LC-USZC4-1325; 57 top, Library of Congress, Reproduction Number: LC-USZC4-11658; 57 bottom, Wellcome Library, London: http://creativecommons.org/licenses/by/4.0/: note: original background removed; 58, © The Keasbury-Gordon Photograph Archive/Alamy Stock Photo; 60, Portrait of a Mpongwe woman, Gabon, Libreville, Photographer: Francis W. Joaque, 1875 to 1885. © Museum der Kulturen Basel. (F) III 23593. DEP. G. PASSAVANT I. (red album) ALL RIGHTS RESERVED; 61, © iStock.com/duncan1890; 64, Library of Congress, Reproduction Number: LC-DIG-nclc-03701; 65, Library of Congress, Reproduction Number: LC-USZC2-3131; 66, © Chronicle/Alamy Stock Photo; 67, Library of Congress, Reproduction Number: LC-DIG-cwpb-04155; 69 top, Library of Congress, Reproduction Number: LC-USZ62-119897; 69 bottom, Library of Congress, Reproduction Number: LC-USZ62-64712; 70, © Jeffrey Banke/Dreamstime.com; 72 left, Library of Congress, Reproduction Number: LC-USZ62-85874; 72 right, Library of Congress, Reproduction Number: HABS ALA,54-MEM,2-B—1; 73, Library of Congress, Reproduction Number: LC-USZ62-94390; 75, © Pictorial Press Ltd/Alamy Stock Photo; 76, Library of Congress, Reproduction Number: LC-USZC4-1062; 77, Clipart.com; 79, © The Advertising Archives/Alamy Stock Photo; 80, Anibal Trejo/Bigstock.com; 83, Library of Congress, Reproduction Number: LC-USZC4-14685; 86, © Homer Sykes Archive/Alamy Stock Photo; 88, © iStock.com/vicnt; 89 both, © Zkruger/Dreamstime.com; 90, © frans lemmens/Alamy Stock Photo; 94 top, © Olha Rohulya/Dreamstime.com; 94 bottom, © iStock.com/EdStock/Photo by Paula Bronstein; 95, © Grigor Atanasov/Dreamstime.com; 97, back cover, © iStock.com/Antagain; 99, © Vav63/Dreamstime.com; 101, © afin/Alamy Stock Photo.

Selected Sources

Arvigo, Rosita, and Nadine Epstein. *Spiritual Bathing: Healing Rituals and Traditions from Around the World.* Berkeley, CA: Celestial Arts, 2003.

Bushman, Richard L., and Claudia Bushman. "The Early History of Cleanliness in America." *Journal of American History 74* (March 1988): 1213–38.

Carcopino, Jerome. *Daily Life in Ancient Rome.* Trans. E. O. Lorimer. New York: Penguin, 1991.

Clark, Scott. *Japan: A View from the Bath.* Honolulu: University of Hawaii Press, 2004.

Classen, Constance, David Howes, and Anthony Synnot. *Aroma: The Cultural History of Smell.* New York: Routledge, 1994.

Connolly, Peter, and Hazel Dodge. *The Ancient City: Life in Classical Athens and Rome.* Oxford: Oxford University Press, 1998.

Corbin, Alain. *The Foul and the Fragrant: Odor and the French Social Imagination.* Trans. Miriam L. Kochan, Roy Porter, and Christopher Prendergast. Cambridge, MA: Harvard University Press, 1986.

De Bonneville, Françoise. *The Book of the Bath.* Trans. Jane Brenton. New York: Rizzoli, 1998.

Duby, Georges. *A History of Private Life, II: Revelations of the Medieval World.* Trans. Arthur Goldhammer. Cambridge, MA: Harvard University Press, 1988.

Elias, Norbert. *The Civilizing Process: The History of Manners.* Trans. Edmund Jephcott. Oxford: Basil Blackwell, 1978.

Fagan, Garrett G. *Bathing in Public in the Roman World.* Ann Arbor, MI: University of Michigan Press, 1999.

Flanders, Judith. *The Victorian House.* New York: HarperCollins, 2003.

Giedion, Sigfried. *Mechanization Takes Command: A Contribution to Anonymous History.* New York: W. W. Norton, 1969.

Goubert, Jean-Pierre. *The Conquest of Water: The Advent of Health in the Industrial Age.* Trans. Andrew Wilson. Princeton, NJ: Princeton University Press, 1989.

Hamilton, Gerry. "Why We Need Germs." *The Ecologist Report* (June 2001), www.mindfully.Org/Health/We-Need-Germs.html.

Hoy, Suellen. *Chasing Dirt: The American Pursuit of Cleanliness.* New York: Oxford University Press, 1996.

Ierley, Merritt. *The Comforts of Home: The American House and the Evolution of Modern Convenience.* New York: Three Rivers Press, 1999.

Ladd, Brian K. "Public Baths and Civic Improvement in Nineteenth-Century German Cities." *Journal of Urban History* 14, no. 3 (May 1988): 372–93.

Lam, Vincent, and Colin Lee. *The Flu Pandemic and You: A Canadian Guide.* Toronto: Doubleday Canada, 2009.

Miner, Horace. "Bodily Ritual Among the Nacirema." *American Anthropologist* 58 (1956): 503–7.

Perrot, Michelle, ed. *A History of Private Life, IV: From the Fires of Revolution to the Great War.* Trans. Arthur Goldhammer. Cambridge, MA: Harvard University Press, 1990.

Salkin, Allen. "Germs Never Sleep." *The New York Times,* November 5, 2006.

Schaub, Bianca, Roger Lauener, and Erika von Mutius. "The Many Faces of the Hygiene Hypothesis." *Journal of Allergy and Clinical Immunology* 117 (2006): 1969–77.

Sivulka, Juliann. *Soap, Sex, and Cigarettes: A Cultural History of American Advertising.* Belmont, CA: Wadsworth, 1998.

———. *Stronger Than Dirt: A Cultural History of Advertising Personal Hygiene in America, 1875–1940.* Amherst, NY: Humanity Books, 2001.

Specter, Michael. "Germs Are Us. Bacteria Make Us Sick. Do They Also Keep Us Alive?" *The New Yorker,* October. 22, 2012. www.newyorker.com/magazine/2012/10/22/germs-are-us.

Vigarello, Georges. *Concepts of Cleanliness: Changing Attitudes in France Since the Middle Ages.* Trans. Jean Birrell. Cambridge, UK: Cambridge University Press, 1988.

Vinikas, Vincent. *Soft Soap, Hard Sell: American Hygiene in an Age of Advertisement.* Ames, IA: Iowa State University Press, 1992.

Williamson, Jefferson. *The American Hotel: An Anecdotal History.* New York: Knopf, 1930.

Yegul, Fikret. *Baths and Bathing in Classical Antiquity.* Cambridge, MA: MIT Press, 1992.

Index